Miniature American Shepherd Activities

Miniature American Shepherd Activities (Tricks, Games & Agility) Includes: Miniature American Shepherd Agility, Easy to Advanced Tricks, Fun Games, plus New Content

Joseph Ball

Copyright © 2023

All rights reserved. Without limiting rights under the copyright reserved above, no part of this publication may be reproduced, stored, introduced into a retrieval system, distributed or transmitted in any form or by any means, including without limitation photocopying, recording, or other electronic or mechanical methods, without the prior written permission of the publisher, except in the case of brief quotations embodied in critical reviews and certain other non-commercial uses permitted by copyright law.

The scanning, uploading, and/or distribution of this document via the Internet or via any other means without the permission of the publisher is illegal and is punishable by law. Please purchase only authorized editions and do not participate in or encourage electronic piracy of copyrightable materials.

A Great Thanks To You

I am truly grateful to you and the many Miniature American Shepherd fans across the globe. You inspired this book to its completion and it is you that we hope it benefits.

We hope that you enjoy the reading that is to come, along with all of the great information.

Wishing you all the best

Once again - Many Thanks.

Table of Contents

Chapter One: "Fetch" Over the Centuries 7
History 7

Chapter Two: Training Methods 10
Clicker Training 10
Dominance Training 12

Chapter Three: Why Teach Your Miniature American Shepherd Tricks? 14

Chapter Four: Understanding the Basics 17
Socialization 17
Obedience Training 19

Chapter Five: Easy Tricks for Your Puppy or Adult Miniature American Shepherd 27
Easy Trick 1 27
Easy Trick 2 28
Easy Trick 3 28
Easy Trick 4 29
Easy Trick 5 30
Easy Trick 6 31
Easy Trick 7 32
Easy Trick 8 32
Easy Trick 9 33
Easy Trick 10 34
Easy Trick 11 35
Easy Trick 12 35
Easy Trick 13 36
Easy Trick 14 37
Easy Trick 15 38

Easy Trick 16 40

Chapter Six: Progressing to Intermediate Level Tricks 42
Intermediate Trick 1 42
Intermediate Trick 2 44
Intermediate Trick 3 45
Intermediate Trick 4 45
Intermediate Trick 5 46
Intermediate Trick 6 47
Intermediate Trick 7 48
Intermediate Trick 8 50
Intermediate Trick 9 51

Chapter Seven: Mastering the Hard Ones 54
Advanced Trick 1 54
Advanced Trick 2 55
Advanced Trick 3 57
Advanced Trick 4 59
Advanced Trick 5 61
Advanced Trick 6 62
Advanced Trick 7 64
Advanced Trick 8 65

Chapter Eight: Mission Impossible? 69
Stubbornness 69
Impatience 69
Physical Problems 70
Mental Slowness 70

Chapter Nine: Games for Both of You 72
The Tissue Game 73
Chase 74
Hide and Seek 74
Bubbles 75

Let's Dance! 76
Ball Roll & Toss 78
Water Fun 78
Surfing 79
Frisbee (Disc) Toss 81
Obstacle Course 83

Chapter Ten: Play is Therapeutic 85
Weight 85
Stress 85
Behavior 86

Chapter Eleven: Agility – The Ultimate in Games 87
Consider Your Miniature American Shepherd 89

Chapter Twelve: Pre-Agility for Puppies 91
Important Points 91
Easy Does It 92

Chapter Thirteen: Agility Basics for Your Adult Miniature American Shepherd 98

Chapter Fourteen: Getting Your Miniature American Shepherd Started 103
Starting with Jumps 109
Getting Used to the Tire 110
Dog Walk 110
A-Frame 112
Tunnel 113
Chute 113
Pause Table 114
Teeter-Totter 115
Weave Poles 117
Putting It All Together 119

Call-Offs... 120

Chapter Fifteen: Getting Involved in Agility 123
Agility Matches 123
Competitive Trials.. 124
Junior Class Agility 124

Chapter Sixteen: The Agility Trial.................................... 126
The Rules 126
Speed Counts 127
How Trials and Meets Are Conducted 128
Faults 129

Chapter Seventeen: Progressing Beyond Standard Agility..133

Chapter Eighteen: Agility Is Not Without Risk 136
Injuries 136
Warm-Up Exercises Before a Trial...................................... 137
Common Agility Injuries 139
Have Fun! 141

Chapter One: "Fetch" Over the Centuries

History

Perhaps because dogs are actually so close to us mentally, they have also proven themselves to be the most malleable of species; malleability being another trait that dogs share with us. Both humans and dogs are able to adapt to new and different situations and activities without very much trouble. The first dogs to be domesticated were obviously used for very practical matters such as hunting or herding, but it undoubtedly wasn't long before dogs began to be seen as companions as well. The intelligence of dogs, which would already have shown itself in the ability for dogs to be trained for hunting, would lead to the teaching of new things, such as tricks.

Human beings love to be entertained. Today we have a myriad of ways to keep our minds occupied, but when you consider how primitive and basic life must have been 30,000 years ago, the ability of dogs to learn tricks must have added greatly to the quality of life. The first 'tricks' that dogs learned to do in those far-off days were those that pertained to hunting. Cave paintings show dogs pursuing game along with their masters, and one even shows a small dog that resembles a Dachshund with large, upright ears, or perhaps a Corgi.

Undoubtedly, the signals given to your Miniature American Shepherds are both verbal and silent, especially if pursing game, and you can actually use hand signals for many of the tricks you teach your Miniature American Shepherd. Our companion Miniature American Shepherds, without being instructed in any way, will look where we point, and several of them will start running in that direction simply from seeing us point.

From learning hunting commands, it certainly would not have been too difficult to teach these early dogs other tricks, which would serve to keep both humans and canines occupied on those long nights, or when the weather was miserable, and they were not out in the field hunting.

Later on, the Ancient Greeks did mention the ability of dogs to do tricks, but unfortunately this was not put in a positive light, and rather looked upon by them as a sign of the wiliness of dogs.

One of the earliest representations of a dog performing tricks is an anonymous painting from around 1380 AD, which shows a shepherd playing an early bagpipe-type instrument while his dog dances before him. For centuries thereafter, few pieces of art showed dogs doing tricks, although dogs were featured not only in hunting scenes from the Middle Ages onward, but also just interacting with people – children and adults are shown with their arms around dogs, and small dogs are to be seen walking around on tables, perhaps sampling some of the fare.

No doubt itinerant entertainers, jesters, Gypsies, and other people have made use of the tricks they taught their dogs to perform to earn a livelihood, regardless that the record is basically mute on them.

Real mention is first made of dogs performing tricks in a book written in the 19th Century – "A History and Description of The Modern Dogs of Great Britain and Ireland (non-sporting division) by Rawdon Lee. In this book, Lee describes a troop of trained poodles that provided entertainment to Queen Anne of England. Dressed as courtiers, the poodles had been given extravagant noble names and danced for the queen and the other observers at court. Rawdon pointed out in his book that these dogs appeared to have been trained to perform their tricks by a combination of kind treatment and patience, a description of what we would today call positive reinforcement.

'Educated' dogs that performed on the street were found and documented not only in England, but also in Paris during the latter part of the 18th and beginning of the 19th Centuries. And these dog shows were the precursor of the performing dogs to be found later in circuses.

Although the concept of the circus had been around since Roman times, it wasn't until 1768 that the first modern circus was offered to the public for entertainment in England. Roman circuses featured gladiatorial contests, horse races, and often combat between humans (usually at a great disadvantage) and wild animals such as lions and bears, and bore very little resemblance to what we consider circuses to be. This first 'modern' circus was actually a horse show, but it was not overly long before the familiar features such as acrobats, clowns, and performing animals, including dogs, were added.

A circus crossed the Atlantic in 1792 to give a performance in Philadelphia which included trained dogs. Circuses, both large and small, seemed to blossom from these beginnings, and dogs 'educated' to perform sometimes very elaborate tricks were to be found in many of them.

More recently well-trained dogs such as Lassie and Benji have demonstrated the extent to which dogs can be taught tricks. Dogs have been trained to do a nearly endless number of tricks, even playing poker like the Yorkshire Terrier, Jilli Dog.

The Miniature American Shepherd can be taught to perform tricks, but always remember that the key to success lies not only in patience, persistence, kindness, and positive reinforcement, but also in accepting the limits of your Miniature American Shepherd, whether mental or physical.

Chapter Two: Training Methods

Over the centuries, countless training methods have been adopted that will hopefully allow your Miniature American Shepherd to be trained easily and effectively. The idea that a dog has to be 'broken' in some way in order to be trained should be considered to be dead and buried, especially as this method generally used harsh punishment to 'break your Miniature American Shepherd's spirit'.

A Miniature American Shepherd that is abused is not only likely to become fearful and stubborn, but also rightfully resentful, and such a Miniature American Shepherd is much more likely to 'turn on its master' than one that has been trained properly. Today, there are much better methods to adopt for effective training that will not only get quicker and more permanent results, but will provide for stronger bonding with your Miniature American Shepherd and a more confident, equable animal.

There are several schools of thought with regards to training, which will be important when you get down to teaching your Miniature American Shepherd tricks. Most of these methods involve the use of positive reinforcement as a means of training your Miniature American Shepherd, and none of them are particularly hard to apply. Most people will probably find that a combination of the two methods will work best; clicker training as a positive reinforcement and a dash of nonviolent dominance training (firm 'No' commands, for example) will help to produce the results you desire.

Clicker Training

One of the most popular training methods in use today is clicker training. The search for a quick and easy way to send a signal to a dog resulted in the use of a clicker. Because the sound is different, and fairly loud, your Miniature American Shepherd will notice it easily over background noises.

Clicker training came into being from research into the effects of positive reinforcement. It is because of the ability of your Miniature American Shepherd to respond to the click more readily that has led to the claim that using a clicker will speed up training by half (rather than just relying on your voice and treats).

When beginning clicker training, the goal is to help your Miniature American Shepherd associate the click with a treat. At this stage, nothing is required of your Miniature American Shepherd except that it open its mouth to receive the treat after hearing the click. You can reinforce with a "Good boy" or "Good girl" if you wish for some additional positive reinforcement. There is no place that is inappropriate for early clicker training: you can click and treat while watching television, while working on the computer, while reading in bed, while sitting in the yard.

Vary the length of time between clicks so your Miniature American Shepherd doesn't get used to receiving a treat regularly. It's best not to conduct 'clicker sessions' more than about 15 minutes at a time, either, which will help to keep the clicker special in your Miniature American Shepherd's mind, rather than just a matter of routine.

When you feel that your Miniature American Shepherd has grasped the connection between the click and the treat, you can start using this training when teaching tricks to your Miniature American Shepherd. The same method will apply, for instance, if you are teaching 'Sit', give the command and if your Miniature American Shepherd sits, click and treat.

Dominance Training

Dominance training has come in for a lot of flack over the last few years. Of course, dominance training that involves physically punishing your Miniature American Shepherd, screaming at your Miniature American Shepherd, depriving your Miniature American Shepherd of food and/or water, or the use of choke or prong collars should be condemned, but I feel that most dominance training does not involve these methods at all.

Ideally, dominance training should include the use of both positive and negative re-enforcers: praise and treats when your Miniature American Shepherd behaves correctly and a firm "No!" when it does not. Striking your Miniature American Shepherd is completely out of line and will be counterproductive; you will either get a fearful, timid Miniature American Shepherd or one that acts up simply to get attention – negative attention is better than no attention at all. You will also be training yourself to lose your temper easily, rather than approaching training equably.

I feel it is a mistake to think that Miniature American Shepherds do not have a natural inclination to a pecking order and that dominance does not play a part in their behavior. Recent studies on wolves claim that there is no dominance in a pack, but watching a video of a senior pack member biting and driving an insubordinate one to the ground certainly looks a good deal like an animal doing its best to preserve the existing dominance hierarchy when a subordinate animal has been getting uppity.

In my own mind, there is no doubt that Miniature American Shepherds feel more secure and confident when they understand their position in the family. This does not denigrate the Miniature American Shepherd at all – would you allow your household to be run by a 2 year old child? As children are considered to be subordinate to their parents, so are Miniature American Shepherds to be considered subordinate to you, the adult owner.

If your Miniature American Shepherd knows it can look up to you for support, comfort, and attention, this will not only make it much more amenable member of the household, but a happier one that will be eager to learn tricks.

Chapter Three: Why Teach Your Miniature American Shepherd Tricks?

It's no secret that a well-trained Miniature American Shepherd is a joy to any household, and one that has been taught to do tricks can not only provide a great deal of amusement to you and your family and friends, but it will also provide your Miniature American Shepherd with mental challenges and the opportunity to bond more closely with you.

When owners complain about their Miniature American Shepherd misbehaving, it often boils down to several things: lack of attention, lack of physical exercise, and lack of mental exercise. Miniature American Shepherds are intelligent and they enjoy learning new things; they enjoy doing some kind of 'work'. Tricks are a great way to address all the issues that may be causing your Miniature American Shepherd to act up. Teaching your Miniature American Shepherd to do tricks helps to also build muscle tone and stamina and can help to substitute for walks when the weather is foul.

In addition to providing both mental and physical exercise for your Miniature American Shepherd, you will also find that you are becoming more responsive and sensitive to it, and this will help to foment a stronger relationship between the two of you. As you progress through the tricks, you will also find that your Miniature American Shepherd 'catches on' more quickly to new tricks. Many Miniature American Shepherds have learned 40 or more tricks without too much difficulty, some of them quite involved and elaborate. However, it doesn't matter whether your Miniature American Shepherd ultimately learns 5 tricks or 50, the point of this book is to help you have fun and bond with your canine companion.

For those of you who are dealing with the sometimes difficult Miniature American Shepherd puppy days – they are absolute bundles of energy and mischief – learning tricks is a good way to channel that hyperactivity constructively. Your Miniature American Shepherd puppy will be receiving the attention it craves and will also be learning how to control its behavior. Remember to keep in mind your puppy's short attention span and never press on once the pup has lost interest. It's a good idea to follow a training session with some unstructured play that the puppy enjoys.

You will be the biggest reason that teaching your Miniature American Shepherd adult or puppy tricks fails – impatience, overwhelming the pet with too many demands, or simply letting instructions slide and expecting your Miniature American Shepherd to pick up immediately on partially forgotten lessons all lead to failure. Literally any Miniature American Shepherd can be taught tricks of some kind, so stay patient, be realistic, stick to a schedule, and use positive reinforcement.

This book is designed to provide you with a way to teach tricks to your Miniature American Shepherd without either of you becoming overwhelmed. Concentrating on a few core tricks, and getting these down pat will be much better than trying to cram dozens of tricks into your Miniature American Shepherd. You might also find our previous book on training your Miniature American Shepherd useful, *"Miniature American Shepherd Training Guide"*, which features: *Miniature American Shepherd Agility Training, Socializing, Housetraining, Obedience Training, Behavioral Training, and much more.*

Always keep in mind that when training your adult or puppy Miniature American Shepherd, it's best to get down to their level where appropriate. Kneeling or squatting down when teaching many of the tricks will help your Miniature American Shepherd to feel more comfortable and relaxed. Consider how enormous and looming we must look to a small Miniature American Shepherd puppy.

When we had our litter of puppies, I made it a point to handle all of them from the time they were born to accustom them to the touch of a human and my voice. They were very relaxed when I did this until their eyes opened. When they saw how enormous I was, all of them were actually afraid, although I had been a second mother to them from their birth. It took them several days to get used to my size, which they soon did, but all of us tend to forget the size differential and the effect it might have on training.

Chapter Four: Understanding the Basics

Before you begin teaching your Miniature American Shepherd tricks, there are certain basic issues that must be addressed if you want your project to be successful. Miniature American Shepherds that are lacking in confidence and that are nervous will be much harder to train than Miniature American Shepherds that feel secure in themselves and around others. Assuming that you are starting with an adult or puppy Miniature American Shepherd that has received no training whatsoever, the first thing to do is to socialize your pet.

Socialization

Socializing your Miniature American Shepherd will involve introducing it to a number of different situations where it will be presented with new experiences. An adult or puppy Miniature American Shepherd can be apprehensive when taken to a new place, and unless you take steps to familiarize your companion, your Miniature American Shepherd can become timid and more difficult to train.

Socializing isn't hard to do, it only requires that you take your pup with you when you go on a walk, especially in a place where it can initially meet only a few people and other pets. It's a good idea to invite people, with or without pet dogs, into your home so that your pup doesn't become overly territorial. Even small puppies will pick up quickly on your reaction to people coming to your home – if you act relaxed when greeting visitors, your pup will, too.

Getting your Miniature American Shepherd used to having other people in your home will not ruin your Miniature American Shepherd's watchdog abilities. Our Miniature American Shepherds take their cue from our actions towards people coming into the home: if they see us greeting the visitors in a friendly manner, they are friendly; an unexpected return visit from the man installing our stove put all three on high alert, with Pip holding the man on one side of the room while the two females stood back and barked in support.

No teeth were involved, Pip was content to simply immobilize the man until relieved of duty. When my sister visited with her friends, we kept our Miniature American Shepherds on leash initially. They closely observed how we reacted to the visitors and when they saw that our reaction was friendly, so was theirs. Our Miniature American Shepherds were relaxed and friendly throughout the visit.

Not surprisingly, the best time to socialize your Miniature American Shepherd is while it is still a puppy. There is a psychological window open when the puppy is 3 to 4 months old during which it is very receptive to meeting and interacting with other people and animals. Positive experiences during this timeframe will be especially valuable in building your Miniature American Shepherd puppy's confidence.

A word of caution – make sure your Miniature American Shepherd puppy is current on its vaccinations before you introduce it to the wide world. There are some very nasty diseases that your puppy could contract, so speak to your vet about establishing a regular vaccination schedule.

Older Miniature American Shepherds can be less receptive to socialization, but this is still not an impossible task, although it might take longer than with a puppy Miniature American Shepherd. While your adult Miniature American Shepherd will not be as likely to want to jump right into play with another dog, you will want to make sure that it doesn't show aggression or fear with humans or dogs.

Start off slowly, with encounters with dogs you know to be friendly. Avoid dog parks where your Miniature American Shepherd might be overwhelmed with the number of dogs and people present, especially if your Miniature American Shepherd is shy. Choose a more relaxing venue, such as a walk where you will meet a few people and their dogs.

Regardless of whether you are trying to socialize a puppy Miniature American Shepherd or an adult Miniature American Shepherd, you want the experience to always be positive. A visit to a dog park that winds up with your Miniature American Shepherd fighting with another dog will not aid in socialization. If your Miniature American Shepherd shows signs of anxiety or aggression, remove it from the situation immediately. Never punish your Miniature American Shepherd for acting like this, however, and either start up more slowly, or if the problem persists, speak to your veterinarian, who may recommend a dog behaviorist. Problem behavior can often be nipped in the bud if addressed quickly, before it becomes a behavioral pattern.

Obedience Training

You are probably eager to jump right into teaching your Miniature American Shepherd tricks, but there is no getting around that your companion will need basic obedience training before it can start learning how to do tricks. Obedience training lays the groundwork for all future training. As with any training, always keep your responses positive; never reprimand or strike the animal if it gets something wrong or refuses to cooperate. Remember the old adage, "You will catch more flies with honey than you will with vinegar".

Most Miniature American Shepherd puppies/adults will require many repetitions before they understand what is wanted of them and can respond correctly. Once again, I encourage you to reference our previous book on training the Miniature American

Shepherd (Miniature American Shepherd Training Guide), available at most book stores including Amazon.

Another thing to keep in mind is a problem many teachers have, whether they are dealing with children or dogs; they seem to think that because they know what the outcome will be that the student will likewise know it automatically. Adult Miniature American Shepherds are considered to have intelligence equal to a 2 or 3 year old human child. It takes dozens of repetitions, in most cases, for a Miniature American Shepherd adult or puppy to learn how to respond correctly to an obedience command. However, nearly every Miniature American Shepherd can be taught these commands: "Come", "Sit", "Stay", "Leave It", and "Down".

You won't need a great deal of equipment for teaching your Miniature American Shepherd these basic commands, which can actually be looked upon as the first tricks your friend will learn – a collar and a long leash, treats, and praise. Keep the learning sessions short, especially when training your Miniature American Shepherd puppy, and break off as soon as your pup starts to lose interest; you will achieve nothing by forcing the animal to continue.

If you find yourself becoming impatient, likewise stop the session and play with your Miniature American Shepherd adult or puppy to help both of you relax. Your pup will pick up on your negative feelings and the effectiveness of your instruction will plummet. Miniature American Shepherds are extremely sensitive to our emotions. Humans and dogs have evolved together over tens of thousands of years, so if you are feeling angry and impatient, your Miniature American Shepherd will know it right away.

Vary where you have your training exercises around the home and yard so that your Miniature American Shepherd pup learns that commands have relevance everywhere, not just in your kitchen or backyard. Alternate commands, too, so that it will be less likely that your trainee will become bored as quickly. Remember too, that some Miniature American Shepherds are much more trainable than others; however, even the most stubborn of Miniature American Shepherds will be able to be trained as long as you are patient. The many different Miniature American Shepherds all have character traits associated with them, but bear in mind that each Miniature American Shepherd is also an individual with its own personality and potential for learning obedience and tricks.

Before starting obedience training, make certain that your Miniature American Shepherd adult or puppy is accustomed to wearing a collar (or harness) and walking on a leash. If you have recently welcomed a Miniature American Shepherd puppy into your home, chances are that it has never had on a collar or been on leash. Our female Miniature American Shepherd puppies objected briefly and dramatically to wearing a collar and being on a leash – they actually threw themselves down onto the ground and thrashed around in seeming despair. We ignored this completely, while trying not to laugh, and literally within minutes, they had gotten over it and had no objection to walking on leash from that point on. Our male pup was more philosophical and walked on the leash without any problem from the first attempt. None of our Miniature American Shepherds have any objection to walking on a leash now.

Another important thing to remember is not to repeat a command that is not obeyed, repeating the command when your Miniature American Shepherd either doesn't understand what you want or is being stubborn will not advance the learning process. Help your adult or puppy Miniature American Shepherd to understand what is wanted, but saying what you want over and over is not teaching the animal to respond to your wishes.

It often helps if 2 people are involved during the training sessions – one to give the command and the other to help the Miniature American Shepherd comply, such as giving it a gentle nudge to get it moving when called. Make sure your pup has its collar and leash on before starting. Take care of elimination needs before starting, too, so that the student is not distracted by bodily demands. Be sure that you have water available at all times.

1. "**Come**". I consider 'Come' to be the first command you should teach to your adult or puppy Miniature American Shepherd. It will probably also be the easiest since your companion will want to be with you as much as possible. Have your helper hold your pet about 7 feet away from you. Kneel down, hold out a treat, and say 'Come'. Give the leash just a slight tug if your Miniature American Shepherd doesn't move, basically to get the pup's attention, but in most cases your pup will come right to you. Make sure you give plenty of praise. Whatever you do, do not drag your Miniature American Shepherd to you, it will immediately dig in its paws and resist and come to look upon training as a punishment.

2. "**Sit**". An easy way to teach your Miniature American Shepherd to sit will involve the use of a treat, as well as a leash. Hold the leash close to the Miniature American Shepherd's collar and hold the treat right above its nose. Move the treat towards your Miniature American Shepherd's back. Because it cannot back up due to the control of the leash, your pup will be forced to sit. As soon as this is accomplished, say 'Sit' and treat. You can also use the command when you see your Miniature American Shepherd sitting already; give the command and treat and praise. If you use either of these methods, it will not be necessary to force your Miniature American Shepherd's hindquarters down, which will always be met with resistance.

3. "**Stay**". This one might be a bit more difficult, due to your Miniature American Shepherd's desire to be with you, but it's not

difficult if you take it slowly. Get your pup into the 'Sit' position, then take a step back, telling your Miniature American Shepherd 'Stay'. If your it remains sitting, you can treat and then take another step back, repeating "Stay' again. Don't be discouraged if this takes a bit longer for your pup to master than 'Come' or 'Sit' because of your Miniature American Shepherd's natural inclination to be with you. To begin with, you should expect your Miniature American Shepherd to break the command fairly readily. As your pup comes to understand the command, you should increase the distance between the both of you.

4. "**Down**". 'Down' can also be somewhat difficult for your Miniature American Shepherd to master because it immediately puts your pup in a subordinate, vulnerable position. This command is useful not only for tricks, but also for keeping your Miniature American Shepherd under control in public places or around children. Shoving your pup down or using the leash to pull your Miniature American Shepherd down is going to make it fearful, there are much better ways to accomplish this. One of the best is ways is to get your pup into a 'Sit', hold a treat in front of its nose, and gradually lower the treat to the floor. As soon as the pup is lying down, say 'Down' and reward. If you find more resistance to this command than to the others, just keep at it, with short sessions.

Some Miniature American Shepherds will be more likely to learn this if you place a pad on the floor first, it simply makes it more comfortable to lie down. You Miniature American Shepherd should learn 'Down' more quickly if you get yourself down to its level by kneeling or squatting. Keeping your face near theirs while doing this helps too.

Note: If your Miniature American Shepherd nips at your face when you bring it close, contact a dog behaviorist immediately; your pup is probably exhibiting fear aggression and this could develop into a serious problem.

5. **"Leave It"** or **"No"**. All of us who own Miniature American Shepherds have been faced with situations where they have picked up something awful or dangerous from the ground, and we fear that we may not be able to get to them quickly enough to remove it from their mouth. However, it's not very hard to teach your Miniature American Shepherd how to leave something alone, and learning this could prevent it from becoming ill or even dying. Miniature American Shepherds can try to eat dangerous things such as bones, dead animals, or garbage.

It's not unknown, unfortunately, for poison to be left out for dogs, or rodents that have been poisoned can kill your Miniature American Shepherd if it eats one (most rodenticides cause the mouse or rat to want to get outside which will make the corpse available to your pet).

For this lesson, you will need a leash and some treats. Leash your Miniature American Shepherd, holding the leash close to your side, then place a treat on the floor several feet from your pup. When your Miniature American Shepherd makes a move towards the treat, hold the leash firmly and say 'Leave It' or 'No'. Use a peremptory tone of voice, without shouting, to give this command. Give your pup a treat if it refrains from going towards the lure, then put another treat down on the floor. Use toys as well as treats to train your Miniature American Shepherd. Once your pup has mastered this step, you can tell it 'No' or 'Leave It' when it has something in its mouth, and by this point your Miniature American Shepherd should release whatever it is. Be sure to praise your pooch for every success and ignore any missteps. We always have used 'No' because it's short and sharp and gets your Miniature American Shepherd's attention right away; I think it rather resembles the peremptory bark that a pup might get from its mother when it was doing something unwanted.

Once you have completed your Miniature American Shepherd's basic training, you should go to the more advanced obedience command 'Heel'. While this can be somewhat difficult to teach your pooch, it will also be invaluable not only with dog tricks, but also with games and agility.

6. **"Heel"**. 'Heel' is usually considered to be the hardest basic obedience command to teach your pet. All of us have had the joy of being dragged along by an overly enthusiastic dog, and it can sometimes feel as if your arm is going to be pulled out of its socket. Not only does this take the fun out of walks for the human partner, but can also make it more likely that your Miniature American Shepherd will get in trouble with another dog or a person. Do not try to teach 'Heel' with one of those retractable dog leashes, use a leather or nylon leash that is approximately 6" long.

Do not use a choke or prong collar, a flat collar is all that is needed; you can seriously damage your Miniature American Shepherd's throat using prong or choke collars. Stand with your Miniature American Shepherd on your left side and start to walk, say 'Heel'. Keep the leash short, with your left hand exerting leash control and holding the excess length of leash in your right hand. Stop walking as soon as your Miniature American Shepherd begins to pull, even a little bit. No corrective is needed other than a cessation of motion. Don't jerk the leash or yell, just wait until your Miniature American Shepherd is motionless.

Join your pup and start walking again, repeating the procedure as needed. In most cases, you will have to repeat this many, many times. It can sometimes help to put a little piece of tape on the outside of your left leg to draw your Miniature American Shepherd's attention. Eventually your pooch will walk calmly at your side without pulling.

Now that you and your Miniature American Shepherd have gotten the framework of obedience done, you can probably begin to get going on easy-to-learn tricks for your adult or puppy Miniature

American Shepherd. Dogs in general like to please their masters, so your Miniature American Shepherd will probably be more than willing to work with you to learn tricks. If you are having any problem with basic obedience training, or simply want to help your adult or puppy Miniature American Shepherd become socialized, classes are available that can help with these issues.

Always keep in mind that your Miniature American Shepherd will need 'refreshers' in all of these commands to keep them current.

Chapter Five: Easy Tricks for Your Puppy or Adult Miniature American Shepherd

Now that your Miniature American Shepherd puppy or adult has gotten all the basics down, you can start in on teaching easy tricks. Rather than jumping right to elaborate tricks, regardless of how exciting they may look, beginning with easy, simple tricks will get your Miniature American Shepherd used to learning these new maneuvers and many easy tricks will turn out to be the foundation for more difficult ones. It goes without saying, that if you are using a clicker, to click and treat after every correct response.

Easy Trick 1

Shake

This is one of the easiest tricks to teach and uses one of your Miniature American Shepherd's natural gestures.

1. The first thing to do is to get your Miniature American Shepherd into the 'Sit' position, treat, and praise. Many Miniature American Shepherds will automatically offer you their paw, and if yours does this, take advantage immediately by taking the paw and saying 'Shake'.

2. If your Miniature American Shepherd does not lift its paw automatically, squat down and hold your hand out. More than likely, at some point your pup will move its paw upwards in some way, and this is your cue to take advantage of the situation by taking the paw in your hand and saying 'Shake'.

3. Once your Miniature American Shepherd understands that you will take its paw if it raises it, you can progress to holding out your hand and giving the 'Shake' command. Most dogs will catch on quickly and be sure to treat and praise.

Easy Trick 2

Stack

Most Miniature American Shepherd puppies and adults will 'Stack' by putting both front legs onto an elevated object; perhaps your leg, or maybe the arm of the sofa. If you see your pup in this position, immediately say 'Stack' and reward and treat. If your Miniature American Shepherd doesn't stack on its own, it's easy to teach it to do so.

1. Call your Miniature American Shepherd over to you while sitting on the floor.

2. Pat your leg to encourage your Miniature American Shepherd to touch it with its paw. Treat and praise. Continue to treat and praise every time your Miniature American Shepherd puts its paw onto your leg.

3. Point to your leg now. Your Miniature American Shepherd should put both front paws onto your leg at this point. Say 'Stack' and reward your Miniature American Shepherd.

4. Practice stacking not only with your legs, but also with other objects, such as bricks or books or even an old cookie or candy tin.

5. The final step will be when you can point to an object and say 'Stack' and your Miniature American Shepherd puts both front paws up onto the object. If your Miniature American Shepherd simply seems to be unable to understand what you want, place its front legs where you want them and say 'Stack'.

Easy Trick 3

Jump

Teaching your Miniature American Shepherd to 'Jump' will lay the foundation of more difficult tricks and will also be necessary if you are interested in agility training. The length of your Miniature American Shepherd's legs will determine the maximum height it will be able to jump. Keep your Miniature American Shepherd on a short lead to begin with, although you will dispense with this later.

1. It's best to incrementalize, starting with a stick or bar either on the ground or placed only an inch or two above it. Trot with your Miniature American Shepherd to the bar and lead it over, saying 'Jump' as you do so. Don't be discouraged if your Miniature American Shepherd knocks into the bar to begin with.

2. As your Miniature American Shepherd comes to understand the lesson, you can raise the bar to make the trick more challenging. Every time your Miniature American Shepherd approaches the bar, say 'Jump'. Once your Miniature American Shepherd has learned the trick, remove the lead and let your Miniature American Shepherd jump on its own.

3. You can upgrade this trick by using a hoop: start with the hoop on the ground and gradually raise it, using the 'Jump' command every time your Miniature American Shepherd approaches the hoop. Jumping through a loop you make with your arms is another variation on this theme.

Easy Trick 4

Fetch

All dogs have prey drive, which means that they want to chase and catch what would potentially be food. 'Fetch' uses this prey drive to stimulate your Miniature American Shepherd to go after a designated object and then bring it back to you.

1. Toss one of your Miniature American Shepherd's toys, point to it, and say 'Fetch'. Most Miniature American Shepherds will be eager to go after the toy. Assuming yours does run to the toy and picks it up, praise and treat. If your Miniature American Shepherd just looks at the toy, run after it yourself, it will help to

excite it and show it what is needed. Don't move on to the next step until your Miniature American Shepherd connects the word 'Fetch' with running after the toy.

2. Assuming your Miniature American Shepherd has picked up the toy, say 'Come' to bring your Miniature American Shepherd to you.

3. Once your Miniature American Shepherd is in front of you, say 'Give'. Your Miniature American Shepherd will probably not simply relinquish the toy, so have a treat ready to offer in exchange. Do not engage in a tug of war over the toy. Hand feeding of your Miniature American Shepherd, from the time it was a puppy will make it much more likely that the toy will be released without fuss, as your Miniature American Shepherd will be used to having your hands near its mouth (hand feeding greatly reduces food aggression, too).

Easy Trick 5

Give

Mentioned in the trick above, 'Give' will be much easier to teach if you have been hand feeding your puppy or adult Miniature American Shepherd. Isolating your Miniature American Shepherd with a dish when it's kibble time only fosters feelings of possessiveness in your Miniature American Shepherd and makes it less likely that it will relinquish objects from its mouth. When hand feeding your puppy or adult Miniature American Shepherd, take the food out of its mouth every so often, praising the pup for letting you do so and immediately giving the tidbit back.

We have hand fed our Miniature American Shepherds from their puppy days and have never had a problem in taking things from their mouths if necessary (even food) and have never been bitten by them either, and not a hint of a growl. If you have a Miniature

American Shepherd that already suffers from food aggression or bites when you get near its food, see your veterinarian or an animal behaviorist before working on 'Give'.

1. Throw a toy and tell your Miniature American Shepherd to 'Fetch'.

2. Once your Miniature American Shepherd has the toy, say 'Come'.

3. When your Miniature American Shepherd has come to you, take the toy while saying 'Give'. Holding a treat up to your Miniature American Shepherd's nose will prompt it to open its mouth to get the treat, thereby releasing the toy. Give your Miniature American Shepherd the treat and praise it.

4. Repeat these steps several times until your Miniature American Shepherd allows you to take the object out of its mouth without problem; keep the treat in sight, and smell, and your Miniature American Shepherd will be happy for you to remove the object.

Easy Trick 6

Drop

This is built on the above 'Give' trick. As soon as your Miniature American Shepherd gives you whatever it has fetched reliably, you can move on to 'Drop'.

1. Follow the 'Fetch' sequence.

2. When your Miniature American Shepherd brings the object to you, don't take it out of its mouth.

3. Hold a treat to your Miniature American Shepherd's nose; sooner or later, your Miniature American Shepherd will let go of the object to get the treat.

4. As soon as the object is released, say 'Drop'. Give your Miniature American Shepherd the treat.

Easy Trick 7

Pull

This should be very easy to teach, as nearly every dog alive loves a tug-of-war.

1. Using a rope toy or just a piece of rag with a knot in it, let your Miniature American Shepherd take one end in its mouth. Tug on your end and it's almost a 100% chance that your Miniature American Shepherd will begin tugging on the other. Whenever your Miniature American Shepherd gives a tug, say 'Pull' and praise. This trick will come in useful for more involved tricks.

2. Tie the rag or rope onto a door handle and show it to your Miniature American Shepherd. If you've been playing tug-of-war with your Miniature American Shepherd it will probably take the rag into its mouth, if not, hold the rag out to it.

3. As soon as your Miniature American Shepherd has the cloth in its mouth, say 'Pull'. Treat your Miniature American Shepherd as soon as it pulls even a little bit. This trick is useful not only for opening doors, but can also be used for fetching cans from the fridge.

Easy Trick 8

Sit Pretty (Beg)

Certainly one of the old favorites, you'll find it isn't very difficult to teach your Miniature American Shepherd to 'Sit Pretty'. If you haven't taught your Miniature American Shepherd to 'Sit', you will have to go back and teach that before starting this trick.

1. Tell your Miniature American Shepherd to 'Sit'.

2. Hold a treat in front of your Miniature American Shepherd's nose and slowly raise it up higher. If your Miniature American Shepherd breaks the 'Sit', start over again.

3. As your Miniature American Shepherd tries to get the treat, it will position itself in an upright sitting position, with its front legs off the ground. Give your Miniature American Shepherd the treat now. Repeat this until your Miniature American Shepherd does it reliably.

4. Now it's time to add the command. You may want to use either 'Beg' or 'Pretty' so as to avoid confusion with the 'Sit' command. Chose one command and use it consistently. Make certain to treat your Miniature American Shepherd as soon as it performs the trick reliably as well as praising your Miniature American Shepherd verbally. You can dispense with the treat once your Miniature American Shepherd responds correctly, but continue with verbal praise.

Easy Trick 9

Crawl

This trick will actually come in handy later on if you want to participate in agility with your Miniature American Shepherd, and could help your Miniature American Shepherd master the both the open and collapsed tunnel.

1. Tell your Miniature American Shepherd 'Down'.

2. Put a treat on the floor in front of your Miniature American Shepherd, about 1 foot away, but cover it with your hand.

3. Lift up your hand a bit to show your Miniature American Shepherd the treat and say 'Crawl'. To begin with, your Miniature American Shepherd will undoubtedly jump up to get the treat. Return it to the 'Down' position and hide a treat beneath your hand again.

4. Keeping your hand hovering over the treat will help keep your Miniature American Shepherd's interest close to the ground and more likely to scoot along in a crawl rather than get up.

5. As soon as your Miniature American Shepherd is actually crawling towards the treat, pull it back further to keep it crawling. If your Miniature American Shepherd gets back onto its feet at this stage, it could be because you are pulling the treat back too quickly. Slow down until your Miniature American Shepherd really gets the hang of the trick.

Easy Trick 10

Nose Balance

This is a fairly easy trick to teach most Miniature American Shepherds. However, you may be presented with some challenges at times but remember that the secret to success is patience and perseverance. Before starting actual training, make sure that your Miniature American Shepherd is comfortable with you putting your hands on its muzzle. If this is fairly new to your puppy or adult Miniature American Shepherd, take a bit of time to make sure your pup isn't skittish when something comes near its face; instinct tells your Miniature American Shepherd that that is where the teeth are. Once that has been accomplished, you can begin to teach the trick. You can use treats or objects as the balancing item, although your Miniature American Shepherd would probably prefer the treat.

1. 'Sit' followed by 'Stay' is a good way to begin. Praise your Miniature American Shepherd.

2. If you are using an object, make sure that it's lightweight. Place the treat or object close to your Miniature American Shepherd's stop, which will help to hold it in place; it's probably better not to start with a ball which might just roll off your Miniature American Shepherd's nose. Treat and praise. Use the cue 'Balance'.

3. Leave the object on your Miniature American Shepherd's nose for only a few seconds and remove it before your Miniature American Shepherd starts to act uncomfortable.

4. You can leave the object on for longer and longer periods as your Miniature American Shepherd becomes used to it. Always remember to give a treat and praise your Miniature American Shepherd, and never leave the object on for an extended period of time.

Easy Trick 11

Speak

This trick is not only easy to teach your Miniature American Shepherd, but can also help to prevent nuisance barking as your pup will learn only to bark when told to do so.

1. As soon as your puppy or adult Miniature American Shepherd barks, say 'Speak' and praise and treat.

2. Repeat this step and then try giving the command while your pup is quiet.

3. If you are lucky enough to have a very quiet Miniature American Shepherd, you can often get it to bark by introducing a strange noise, such as someone pounding on the front door or shouting outside. This will often stimulate your Miniature American Shepherd's protective instincts enough to cause it to bark.

4. As your Miniature American Shepherd comes to understand the 'Speak' command, put your Miniature American Shepherd into 'Sit' before giving it. This will make it easier to teach more difficult tricks later on.

Easy Trick 12

Bow

This trick takes advantage of your Miniature American Shepherd's natural invitation to play. When dogs want to play with you or just another dog, they lower their front quarters while leaving their rear up in the air. Just build on this inclination to have your Miniature American Shepherd 'Bowing' on cue.

1. Wait until you see your Miniature American Shepherd in the play position and say 'Bow' and treat.

2. Every time your Miniature American Shepherd indicates it wants to play, say 'Bow' and give your Miniature American Shepherd a treat.

3. After several repetitions, try saying 'Bow' while your Miniature American Shepherd is simply standing in front of you. Don't expect a correct response immediately, although some Miniature American Shepherds might surprise you.

4. If your Miniature American Shepherd simply doesn't seem to get the message, try leading its front quarters down to the ground by holding a treat in front of its nose and lowering it to the floor.

5. In case your Miniature American Shepherd goes into the 'Down' position with its entire body on the floor, have a helper hold its hindquarters up while the front are lowering. Remember to say 'Bow' as you work on this and don't stint on treats and praise.

Easy Trick 13

Salute

This is another easy trick that is based on your Miniature American Shepherd's natural actions. Keep in mind that this 'Salute' will be performed with one of the hind legs. This is an amusing trick that I taught to our male Miniature American Shepherd, and he developed real pride in kicking out his right hind leg and holding it there in a very nice salute. As you know, most Miniature American Shepherds will kick at the ground with their hind legs after going to the bathroom, and it is just this action that you will be using to teach your Miniature American Shepherd to salute.

Both male and female Miniature American Shepherds can learn this without much trouble, and from my experience, they seem to enjoy doing it, too. This might be a good trick if you have a family member returning from military service; he or she will probably be delighted to be greeted with a salute.

1. After your Miniature American Shepherd has finished its business and has started to kick out, say 'Salute'. Treat your Miniature American Shepherd.

2. Repeat this command every time your Miniature American Shepherd does it, and it won't be very long before your Miniature American Shepherd comes to associate the word with the action.

3. Once your Miniature American Shepherd seems to connect the word with kicking out its hind leg, give the 'Salute' command. Undoubtedly your Miniature American Shepherd will not understand what you want, but repeat the command several times. Don't overdo this, if there isn't success after 2 or 3 tries, leave off for the time being, and wait for the next trip outside.

4. Any slight quiver of the hind leg should be looked upon as a victory and rewarded. It should not be too long before your Miniature American Shepherd will give you a salute upon command.

Easy Trick 14

Spin

Spinning is something like a dog chasing its tail, but instead of it being a spontaneous action, it is now a trick to be done upon cue. Some dogs actually spin naturally, we had a dog quite some time ago who would spin around in circles when she got excited.

1. Hold a treat right in front of your Miniature American Shepherd's nose.

2. Move the treat towards your Miniature American Shepherd's right shoulder, keeping it as close as possible to its body. Your Miniature American Shepherd should turn in a tight circling motion to try to get the treat.

3. Keep moving the treat around until you have completed a complete rotation, then say 'Spin' and give your Miniature American Shepherd the treat.

4. Use this same procedure to have your Miniature American Shepherd go around several times, slowly at first, then upping the speed. Remember to tell your Miniature American Shepherd to 'Spin' as you move the treat.

5. Try causing your Miniature American Shepherd to move simply by moving your hand the same way you moved the treat, your Miniature American Shepherd will probably just follow your hand.

6. This is a good treat to teach using both verbal and hand signals. In addition to saying 'Spin', you can also make a circular motion with your hand. Before long your Miniature American Shepherd will probably be spinning away just on command. Always remember to treat and praise.

Easy Trick 15

High Five

This might be looked upon as the modern world's 'Shake' and is just as easy to teach as shake is. It utilizes your Miniature American Shepherd's natural inclination to paw at things, and might be very amusing if you have two dogs and they are taught to 'High Five' one another. This trick depends on utilizing your Miniature American Shepherd's sense of smell to get results, so be sure to have some highly odorous treats that your Miniature

American Shepherd really likes, such as a piece of meat or cheese ready.

1. Put your Miniature American Shepherd into the 'Sit' position and give a treat.

2. Place one of the treats into your hand and make a fist. Even though your Miniature American Shepherd will not be able to see the treat, it will certainly be able to smell it.

3. Put your hand in front of your Miniature American Shepherd, slightly below its nose. Your hand should be only a few inches from your Miniature American Shepherd at this point.

4. Inevitably, your Miniature American Shepherd will try to sniff at your hand to get the treat, but you should totally ignore this. Don't even say 'No'.

5. When attempting to sniff gets no results, most Miniature American Shepherds will paw at your hand. Give your Miniature American Shepherd the treat and praise it.

6. Repeat the above step until your Miniature American Shepherd consistently paws at your fist, rather than sniffing at it.

7. Now, open your hand, keeping the palm up and hold it just where you were holding your fist. Most Miniature American Shepherds will paw at your open hand. If your Miniature American Shepherd doesn't, then just go back to the fist, but with nothing in it, until your Miniature American Shepherd paws at your open hand. You may well have to go back and forth several times.

8. Once your Miniature American Shepherd is pawing reliably at your open palm, put it into the correct position for a high five. As soon as your Miniature American Shepherd taps your palm, say 'High Five' and treat. It shouldn't be long before all your Miniature American Shepherd has to do to give you a 'High Five' is to see your palm presented.

Easy Trick 16

Kiss

As long as you don't mind getting licked on your face, this is a rather endearing and easy trick to teach to your Miniature American Shepherd. Make sure that your Miniature American Shepherd is comfortable having your face close to its face, some Miniature American Shepherds are skittish about this, especially if you have a Miniature American Shepherd that you adopted as an adult. However, as long as you don't mind your Miniature American Shepherd's tongue and breath, and both of you are calm when in close proximity, you may enjoy learning this trick.

Keep in mind that even if you enjoy getting a big, juicy kiss from your Miniature American Shepherd, visitors or other family members may not find the trick to be very amusing, so ask the other person whether or not they do want a kiss from your Miniature American Shepherd before directing your Miniature American Shepherd to do so.

1. Put a small smear of something like strawberry jam, peanut butter, or gravy on your cheek or even the end of your nose.

2. Put your face at the level of your Miniature American Shepherd's face. Your Miniature American Shepherd will, of course, be attracted to the lure and lick.

3. When your Miniature American Shepherd does lick your face, say 'Kiss'. This will probably be one of the easiest tricks to teach your Miniature American Shepherd, and you will soon be able to dispense with the lure and just rely on the cue to get results.

4. Depending on how liquid your Miniature American Shepherd's mouth is, you may want to have a tissue ready to mop up after the kiss.

These basic, easy-to-learn and easy-to-teach tricks can now form the foundation of more difficult tricks to teach your Miniature

American Shepherd. You and your Miniature American Shepherd are now very comfortable working with one another and are really functioning as a team. Of course, if you are satisfied with this level, it's perfectly acceptable to remain here, there is nothing to demand that you go on to tricks of an intermediate difficulty, the whole point is to have fun with your Miniature American Shepherd, not to be in any kind of competition.

Chapter Six: Progressing to Intermediate Level Tricks

Hopefully you and your puppy or adult Miniature American Shepherd have had a lot of fun learning the easy tricks, and both of you might well be eager to get started on intermediate tricks. These will add a bit of complexity and interest, but are not beyond the ability of most Miniature American Shepherds to learn.

Teaching your Miniature American Shepherd obedience and then easy tricks will not only have strengthened the bond between you, but both of you will be able to work more effectively as a team – you have both learned to respond to one another more effectively, picking up even subtle cues of facial expression or body language. Intermediate tricks will add another dimension to your Miniature American Shepherd's activities, and the challenge they pose will help to keep your Miniature American Shepherd stimulated and engaged.

Intermediate Trick 1

Push

'Push' is the mirror image of 'Pull' and your Miniature American Shepherd can be taught to do this using its nose or its paws. Adult Miniature American Shepherds may prefer to use their paws, while the smaller puppy Miniature American Shepherds will probably prefer to use their nose (or head). There's no set rule for this so you are free to experiment. Our Miniature American Shepherds always used their heads to butt the door either open or closed. Using this trick, you can train your Miniature American Shepherd to close the door after it comes inside, which is handy at all seasons.

1. You will need to establish a target, such as a small toy or a piece of cloth or paper.

2. Offer the target to your Miniature American Shepherd, allowing your Miniature American Shepherd to sniff it. Tap your finger on the target so that your Miniature American Shepherd will come to associate the sound with the target. Some dogs may paw at it, which is perfectly fine, too. Treat your Miniature American Shepherd. Repeat this until your Miniature American Shepherd will come to the target and touch it reliably.

3. The next step will be to attach the target to a door. Tape the toy, cloth, or paper onto the door at the appropriate level. Tap the target. The door should be just slightly open.

4. Show your Miniature American Shepherd the target, tap the target, and motion your Miniature American Shepherd to go to the door. As soon as your Miniature American Shepherd's nose or paw touches the target, say 'Push'. At this point, it doesn't matter if the door moves or not. Praise your Miniature American Shepherd and treat.

5. You will have to repeat this several times, opening the door a bit wider every time you work at this trick.

6. As your Miniature American Shepherd becomes more adept at this, remove the target and simply tap the door, saying 'Push' as you do so. Treat and praise as soon as your Miniature American Shepherd touches the door.

7. The next step is to tell your Miniature American Shepherd to 'Push' without any other cues than your voice. Stand near the door to get your Miniature American Shepherd to come. By this time, your Miniature American Shepherd will probably understand enough to go to the door and push it closed.

8. Finally, you should be able to give your Miniature American Shepherd the command wherever you are in the room and it will go to the door and close it.

Intermediate Trick 2

Play Dead

This is one of the favorite tricks to teach your Miniature American Shepherd, but is also one where you might encounter some resistance because your Miniature American Shepherd will feel vulnerable. Trust in you has nothing to do with this, it is purely an instinctive reaction, honed by eons of living in the wild. Be patient and calm to help build your Miniature American Shepherd's confidence and trust. You can use both verbal and visual cues for this trick.

1. Give the 'Down' command, either while your Miniature American Shepherd is standing or sitting. Most Miniature American Shepherds will tend to lean one way or another while lying down, so take advantage of this if your Miniature American Shepherd is leaning to the left or right. Praise and treat. Pet your Miniature American Shepherd to help it relax.

2. Once your Miniature American Shepherd seems relaxed, gently push it over onto its side. If your Miniature American Shepherd seems to be panicking, stop immediately and try again after a break. Lying down next to your Miniature American Shepherd can sometimes help it to comply.

3. After a number of repetitions, your Miniature American Shepherd will be able to go from a 'Down' into lying on its side with no problem.

4. Choose the verbal cue for your Miniature American Shepherd, it can be 'You're dead' or 'Play dead'. You can even add a physical cue such as making a chopping motion or holding your hand like a gun.

Intermediate Trick 3

Roll Over

Like 'Play Dead', 'Roll Over' involves using the 'Down' command to begin the trick. You can teach a hand signal while teaching the verbal one, simply make a rolling motion with your hand while cuing your Miniature American Shepherd.

1. Tell your Miniature American Shepherd 'Down'. Praise and treat.

2. Use a treat to draw your Miniature American Shepherd's attention over one of its shoulders – your Miniature American Shepherd's nose will follow the smell.

3. Keep moving the treat farther and farther over, towards your Miniature American Shepherd's back until your Miniature American Shepherd is on its side. Praise and treat.

4. Follow through with the momentum of the treat to encourage your Miniature American Shepherd to roll over onto its back and then onto its other side. At this point say 'Roll Over' and give your Miniature American Shepherd the treat.

5. Several repetitions will teach your Miniature American Shepherd this trick and you can soon dispense with the treat and rely on your verbal command.

Intermediate Trick 4

Get Your Leash

This intermediate trick uses 'Fetch' as its foundation. Don't be surprised, once your Miniature American Shepherd has learned this trick, if it doesn't bring the leash to you unbidden to ask for a walk, however.

1. Place the leash on the floor, step back, and wait for your Miniature American Shepherd to investigate. Praise your Miniature American Shepherd as soon as it noses the leash.

2. Tell your Miniature American Shepherd 'Fetch' and praise and treat when the leash is taken into the mouth.

3. Encourage your Miniature American Shepherd to come to you by slapping your legs or making 'chucking' sounds.

4. When your Miniature American Shepherd brings the leash over to you, praise it, say 'Leash' and treat as soon as your Miniature American Shepherd releases the leash into your hands.

5. You can eliminate the 'Fetch' command and the encouragement for your Miniature American Shepherd to come as soon as your Miniature American Shepherd brings the leash to you reliably, and simply rely on telling your Miniature American Shepherd 'Leash' when it's time for a walk.

Intermediate Trick 5

Play the Piano

No, you won't get any virtuoso performances out of your pup, but you can teach it to plunk away on the piano. Use a bench for your Miniature American Shepherd to sit on, rather than trying to balance on a piano stool, and a padded bench will help with stability.

1. The first step is to teach your Miniature American Shepherd to tap on something with its paws. You can use a disc toy or even a folded up towel. Tell your Miniature American Shepherd 'Sit' and place the target on the floor in front of your Miniature American Shepherd and touch it with your hand.

2. If your Miniature American Shepherd tries to sniff at where you are touching, ignore this and pull your hand away. Try

tapping the target until your Miniature American Shepherd places its paw on it. At this point, be sure to treat and praise.

3. Use the phrase 'Play the Piano' whenever your Miniature American Shepherd taps on the target.

4. Gradually make the target smaller (it will have to be small enough to be placed on the keys of the piano). Use the lid from a small food container or fold up a washcloth.

5. Once your Miniature American Shepherd taps on the smaller target reliably every time you use the cue phrase, it's time to get your pianist to the keyboard.

6. Sit next to your Miniature American Shepherd on the bench to help it feel relaxed and place the target on the keys.

7. Say 'Play the Piano' to get your Miniature American Shepherd to strike on the target. Your Miniature American Shepherd might be a bit startled at the sound to begin with, but most Miniature American Shepherds will accommodate themselves quickly.

8. As soon as your Miniature American Shepherd is striking the target upon command, remove the target and just let your Miniature American Shepherd hit the keys with its paws.

9. One-pawed playing can be expanded to two-pawed playing by putting the target on the keyboard while the first paw is already engaged. Your Miniature American Shepherd will probably catch on quickly to this addition.

Intermediate Trick 6

Leg Weaving

This is fun to do on its own, but will also come in handy if you are interested in agility training. The first thing to do is to train yourself to take long strides – your Miniature American Shepherd will have to move through your legs.

If your Miniature American Shepherd is on the larger side, you can still do this trick by holding one leg out in front of you, bent at the knee, with the foot above the ground. If using this latter technique, you will step down with the foot you had raised, then raise the other one instead and take a long step with that one, too. Once you have gotten your stride down, it's time to start working with your Miniature American Shepherd.

1. Position your Miniature American Shepherd on your left, then take a step forward on your right foot to form a tunnel or arch for your Miniature American Shepherd with your right leg.

2. Hold a treat on the other side of your right leg to get your Miniature American Shepherd to travel through. Say 'Weave' as your Miniature American Shepherd does so. Praise your pup now.

3. Give your Miniature American Shepherd the treat and repeat the instruction using the left leg as the tunnel.

4. Go slowly at first, then gradually increase your striding as your Miniature American Shepherd progresses.

5. With patience, your Miniature American Shepherd will soon be able to weave through your legs as you walk along at a normal pace.

Intermediate Trick 7

Hind Legs Stand

One of our Miniature American Shepherds, and his son, had a natural talent for standing on their hind legs and walking backwards. Both Miniature American Shepherds could navigate a room in reverse with no problem. This was evidently a genetic trait since neither of them had to be taught how to do this, but would do it spontaneously. However, even if your Miniature American Shepherd doesn't have this particular gene, you can teach it to get up onto its hind legs and even walk, either forwards or backwards.

An important thing to keep in mind here is to make sure your Miniature American Shepherd's hips are healthy. Miniature American Shepherds with arthritis or dysplasia should not be taught this trick, it will simply be painful and could make the condition worse. It's probably a good idea to have your veterinarian check your Miniature American Shepherd over, especially its hips and back before starting to teach this trick. Generally, the smaller Miniature American Shepherds have an easier time learning this, but literally any hip healthy Miniature American Shepherd can learn to stand on its hind legs.

1. Tell your Miniature American Shepherd to 'Sit'.

2. Hold a treat above your Miniature American Shepherd's nose and raise it up directly above your Miniature American Shepherd's head. Raising the treat straight up will prevent your Miniature American Shepherd from backing up to try to get the treat.

3. Your Miniature American Shepherd will first sit up on its hind legs, then will raise itself onto its hind feet to reach the treat. Say 'Stand Up' and give your Miniature American Shepherd a treat. You can add a hand signal, gesturing upwards when you give the verbal command.

4. As your Miniature American Shepherd responds to this trick, you can start teaching it to walk towards you while on its hind legs. Holding a treat just above your Miniature American Shepherd's nose and walking slowly backwards will get your Miniature American Shepherd walking upright.

5. Don't overdo this; the muscles in your Miniature American Shepherd's legs and back that keep it upright have to strengthen, and your Miniature American Shepherd's sense of balance must adjust to this new trick.

6. Some Miniature American Shepherds can eventually learn to walk on their back legs for long periods of time and can even learn to dance. It is not unusual to see a Miniature American Shepherd that can dance on its hind legs for several minutes without problem.

Intermediate Trick 8

Find

This trick actually involves 3 steps – 'Sniff', 'Find', and 'Fetch'. 'Sniff', of course, is the easier to teach, but is necessary to proceed on to 'Find'. You will need some treats and whatever object you want your Miniature American Shepherd to find.

As you can see, the tricks are now becoming more complex and challenging, but learning this trick is necessary if you wish to train your Miniature American Shepherd for complicated tricks and tasks in the home.

1. Tell your Miniature American Shepherd to 'Sit'. Hold onto its collar or keep it on leash.

2. Present a treat in front of your Miniature American Shepherd's nose and say 'Sniff'. Don't let your Miniature American Shepherd take the treat.

3. Throw the treat several feet away on the floor, telling your Miniature American Shepherd to 'Stay' to prevent its going right for the treat.

4. Undoubtedly, your Miniature American Shepherd's eyes are riveted on the treat, so release your Miniature American Shepherd and say 'Find'. At this point, your Miniature American Shepherd will not yet associate the command with the action, but several repetitions will serve to teach this trick.

5. Once your Miniature American Shepherd has made the connection between the 'Find' command and going to the treat you can lengthen the distance.

6. Substitute an object for the treat now. Show the object to your Miniature American Shepherd and toss it 4 or 5 feet away. Say 'Find' and release your Miniature American Shepherd. As soon as your Miniature American Shepherd has found the object, say 'Fetch' so that your Miniature American Shepherd will bring it to you.

7. Gradually increase the distance until it has reached a point where your Miniature American Shepherd will not be able to visually find the object.

8. Now it's time to place the object where your Miniature American Shepherd cannot see it. You should begin this by leaving the object on the floor, where your Miniature American Shepherd will come upon it just by walking towards it. The next step will be to conceal the object behind furniture, and then proceed to placing the object in another room.

9. Once the object is out of sight, tell your Miniature American Shepherd to 'Find' and then give the command to 'Fetch'. As long as your Miniature American Shepherd is enjoying itself, this will not be an overly difficult trick for your Miniature American Shepherd to learn.

Intermediate Trick 9

Quiet

Nuisance barking is just that – a nuisance. While barking in your home can be irritating enough, if you live in an apartment house, it could get you evicted if the other tenants are annoyed sufficiently. Even if you live in a detached home, neighbors who live close to you can still be irritated by your barking Miniature American Shepherd, especially if you leave your pooch outside for long periods of time. Your home will be a lot quieter and more peaceful if you teach your Miniature American Shepherd the 'Quiet' command.

If you are interested in teaching your Miniature American Shepherd to be 'Quiet', you are probably getting tired of listening to nonstop barking that can go on almost interminably. Screaming at your Miniature American Shepherd won't help - your Miniature American Shepherd may well think you're just joining in the fun. Once again, like many undesirable behaviors, barking often arises when your Miniature American Shepherd is bored, so working with your Miniature American Shepherd on this in a positive way will ultimately make both of you happier.

1. If you have a problem barker, you probably won't have any difficulty in catching your Miniature American Shepherd in the act. Make sure you have plenty of treats on hand and if you are using a clicker, get ready to click.

2. As soon as there is a break in the barking, praise your Miniature American Shepherd and give it a treat. Do not say anything to your Miniature American Shepherd while it's barking.

3. Your Miniature American Shepherd will soon come to associate a treat with a cessation of barking.

4. Now is the time to introduce the 'Quiet' command, when your Miniature American Shepherd has stopped barking and has gotten a treat.

5. After several repetitions of the above, tell your Miniature American Shepherd 'Quiet' when it's barking. Don't expect miracles the first couple of times, and continue with the rewards during times when your Miniature American Shepherd is not barking. When your Miniature American Shepherd does stop barking when you command it to, be sure to give plenty of treats and praise.

6. The barking habit should eventually fade away as your Miniature American Shepherd gets used to not barking at all.

By now you and your Miniature American Shepherd are on the way to becoming experts and are ready to take on the more difficult tricks. Always remember that you can stop teaching tricks at any level; there is nothing that dictates that you have to continue, the point is to have fun together.

Chapter Seven: Mastering the Hard Ones

The easy and intermediate Miniature American Shepherd tricks have by now laid a solid foundation on which to advance to more difficult and complicated tricks. Both you and your Miniature American Shepherd will now be very well attuned to one another and will be working more as a partnership, rather than just master and dog.

Many of the hard tricks will encompass several stages and will involve tricks that your Miniature American Shepherd has learned already. If you and your Miniature American Shepherd have been proceeding in a positive, upbeat way, your Miniature American Shepherd will probably be eager to start working on more challenging projects.

Advanced Trick 1

Find

Now it's time to take 'Find' to the next phase where you will be teaching your Miniature American Shepherd to find specific objects. Start with one thing you want to find and then add others once your Miniature American Shepherd can reliably find the first.

1. Show your Miniature American Shepherd the object, for instance your slippers (since this seems to be a favorite), and say 'Sniff'. Repeat this several times, giving your Miniature American Shepherd a treat and some praise every time you do so.

2. Once your Miniature American Shepherd has sniffed the slippers adequately, say 'Slippers'. Help your Miniature American Shepherd associate the object with the name by treating and praising.

3. Place the slippers on the floor and say 'Find Slippers'. Hopefully your Miniature American Shepherd will go to the slippers without problem.

4. As soon as your Miniature American Shepherd has picked up one of the slippers, say 'Fetch' to have your Miniature American Shepherd bring the slipper to you. Repeat for the other slipper.

5. Follow the same procedure for any object you want your Miniature American Shepherd to bring to you. Don't overload your Miniature American Shepherd with a laundry list of items to start with, concentrate on a few until your Miniature American Shepherd performs reliably and never forget to praise your Miniature American Shepherd and give it a treat. You can teach your Miniature American Shepherd to identify and find its toys, among other things.

6. Always remember to start teaching your Miniature American Shepherd to 'Find' whatever object by placing it first in full view and gradually lengthening the distance until the object is out of sight completely and your Miniature American Shepherd has to search for it.

Advanced Trick 2

Find Can

If, after a long day at work you just want to relax in front of the television, but realize after sitting down that you don't have anything to drink, you can train your Miniature American Shepherd to bring you a can of your favorite beverage from the refrigerator. You will definitely need hands on work with your Miniature American Shepherd to get this trick down pat, but it is not impossible for a smart Miniature American Shepherd to learn, and will save your weary feet once your Miniature American Shepherd understands what is required of it.

This trick will require the use of several previous tricks including 'Find', 'Pull', 'Come', 'Push' and will require patience on your part. Because of the complexity of this trick, your Miniature American Shepherd will have to learn the proper sequence for it to be successful, so be patient and have plenty of treats on hand.

1. Tie a piece of cloth or a rag to the refrigerator handle

2. Take your Miniature American Shepherd to the refrigerator and point out the rag. Tell your Miniature American Shepherd 'Pull'. If your Miniature American Shepherd has mastered this trick, it will take the rag and pull to open the door. As soon as the refrigerator door is open, praise your Miniature American Shepherd and treat.

3. Now, you have to familiarize your Miniature American Shepherd with the can. Take a can of beverage out of the refrigerator and put it on the floor in front of your Miniature American Shepherd. Say 'Can'. Use a cold can to get your Miniature American Shepherd used to the feel of the cold can in its mouth. Your Miniature American Shepherd may lick the can, which is perfectly all right.

4. Touch the can and say 'Find Can'. If your Miniature American Shepherd doesn't pick the can up in its mouth, put the can into your Miniature American Shepherd's mouth yourself. Do not pry open your Miniature American Shepherd's jaws to do this, chances are that your Miniature American Shepherd will just take the can when you offer it. Make sure you praise your Miniature American Shepherd as soon as the can is in its mouth.

5. Place the can in the fridge on the lowest shelf (if you use the door for cans, likewise place it on the lowest slot). Point to the can or tap it with your finger and say 'Find Can'. Once your Miniature American Shepherd will reliably take the can off the shelf, it's time for the next step.

6. Now your lessons teaching your Miniature American Shepherd to close door will come in handy as you tell your Miniature American Shepherd to 'Push' while tapping on the refrigerator door. Praise your Miniature American Shepherd.

7. Go to wherever you enjoy sitting, while your Miniature American Shepherd still has the can in its mouth and say 'Come'. Your Miniature American Shepherd should come to where you are and you can take the can out of its mouth. Be lavish with the praise.

8. This is a very difficult and involved trick to teach your Miniature American Shepherd, but it can be done as long as you are willing to put in the time and have the patience to teach it. You will need to go through the steps quite a few times with most Miniature American Shepherds.

9. Remember that your Miniature American Shepherd will have to learn that the 'Find Can' command actually is only the trigger for a number of other actions that will have to be followed.

10. Once you feel confident that your Miniature American Shepherd has mastered all the steps, sit down and tell your Miniature American Shepherd 'Find Can', then sit back and relax with a nice, cool drink.

Advanced Trick 3

Jump Rope

You can teach this in collaboration with another person to hold one end of the rope, or you can do it by yourself by tying one end of the rope to a stationary object. This is one of the hardest tricks to learn, but one that will be rewarding for both you and your Miniature American Shepherd. Don't start teaching this until your puppy has basically stopped growing as beginning too early could cause damage to the pup's hips. In order to do this trick, your Miniature American Shepherd should already know

'Jump' and 'Stand Up'. If your Miniature American Shepherd is unfamiliar with these, go back and teach these first.

Where you conduct your lessons will depend upon the size/age of your Miniature American Shepherd. For your smaller pooch, you could place it on a table to make it easier for both of you, and for a larger one, you could teach your lesson on the floor.

Place a small rug with low pile and rubber backing (a bathmat works very well) on the table or a bare floor to provide good traction for your Miniature American Shepherd's feet. It might also be a good idea to make sure that your Miniature American Shepherd's claws are adequately trimmed as long nails can get caught in rug pile and can make it hard for your Miniature American Shepherd to stand up or jump.

The only equipment you will need for this trick is a jump rope. Because of the complexity of this trick, you should have a plentiful supply of treats on hand.

1. Your Miniature American Shepherd should be introduced to the rope by swinging it back and forth in front of it. Let your Miniature American Shepherd sniff the rope, but don't let it bite it. Treat and praise.

2. Once your Miniature American Shepherd is comfortable with the moving rope, position the rope on the floor behind your Miniature American Shepherd, give it a nearly full rotation to end up stationary at your Miniature American Shepherd's front feet. At this point, say 'Jump' and as your Miniature American Shepherd jumps, move the rope beneath its feet. Praise and treat.

3. Flip the rope like this over and over, saying 'Jump' each time the rope appears in front of your Miniature American Shepherd's front feet. In time your Miniature American Shepherd will begin to jump as soon as it sees the rope approaching its feet. Once your Miniature American Shepherd has mastered this part of the instructions, it's time to move onto the next.

4. Now it's time to get your Miniature American Shepherd to stand up and jump when the rope comes around. The first thing to do is give the 'Stand Up' command. Praise and treat.

5. As you did when your Miniature American Shepherd was in a normal position, flip the rope from in back of your Miniature American Shepherd to just before its hind feet and say 'Jump'. Quickly move the rope to the back of your Miniature American Shepherd's feet (your Miniature American Shepherd is on its hind legs now, so don't linger).

6. Repeat flipping the rope and saying 'Jump' until your Miniature American Shepherd is able to do this reliably. Keep the rope jumping slow at first, and gradually speed it up as your Miniature American Shepherd gains skill and its balance improves.

Advanced Trick 4

Count

When your Miniature American Shepherd learns this trick, it will definitely look like a canine genius! This trick will combine the 'Speak' trick with eye and hand signals from you. The complicated nature of this trick means that you will probably have to spend considerable time working on it, but it will definitely amaze your friends when your Miniature American Shepherd does arithmetic for them. Remember to remain patient and stick with it.

1. Tell your Miniature American Shepherd to 'Sit' and position yourself so that your face is directly in front of your Miniature American Shepherd's face. You won't have to be this close after your Miniature American Shepherd has learned the trick.

2. Hold up your right hand while holding a treat in your left.

3. Look into your Miniature American Shepherd's right eye, making sure that you are both making eye contact with each other.

4. Tell your Miniature American Shepherd to 'Speak' and give it the treat as soon as your Miniature American Shepherd does so. Make certain that your Miniature American Shepherd is still looking you in the eye. Repeat this several times so that your Miniature American Shepherd comes to associate barking with your eye contact.

5. The next step will have you telling your Miniature American Shepherd to 'Speak', but now you will avert your eyes. Let your right hand drop down a bit, too. The point here is to let your Miniature American Shepherd know that when you let your hand fall and avert your eyes, that there is to be no more barking. Treat when your Miniature American Shepherd cooperates. Repeat this and treat whenever your Miniature American Shepherd stops barking when you avert your eyes and drop your hand.

6. Once your Miniature American Shepherd understands that one bark is sufficient when you look away, it's time to train your Miniature American Shepherd to bark twice. Position yourself as above and tell your Miniature American Shepherd to 'Speak'. Repeat the command if your Miniature American Shepherd stops after one bark. Keep eye contact until 2 barks have been given. Some Miniature American Shepherds will bark too much and some will bark too little, but by persevering, you will eventually teach your Miniature American Shepherd to cease barking as soon as you avert your eyes and drop your hand.

7. Build on the number of barks required using both eye and hand signals, always remembering to treat and praise after a success.

8. When your Miniature American Shepherd is reliably barking to your cues, stop using the hand signal and rely on your eyes only.

9. Now it's time to add the math: ask your Miniature American Shepherd how much is 1 + 1? Then tell your Miniature American Shepherd 'Speak'.

10. As soon as your Miniature American Shepherd barks twice, avert your eyes. You can use addition, subtraction, multiplication, and division to show off your Miniature American Shepherd's education, but try to keep the numbers on the low side to make it easier for your Miniature American Shepherd and make it more likely that the trick will be a success.

Advanced Trick 5

Grip Object

While you will be training your Miniature American Shepherd with a lightweight object that it can grasp easily, once your Miniature American Shepherd has learned how to grip an object, you can use any number of things, including dolls or toys. A plastic, personal-size water bottle is a good choice, but because it's slippery, you might find it easier for your Miniature American Shepherd to grip this if you tape a lightweight piece of cloth around it. You will use the word 'Grip' for this trick.

1. Show the bottle to your Miniature American Shepherd and praise as soon as your Miniature American Shepherd touches its nose to the bottle. This will familiarize your Miniature American Shepherd with the object.

2. Repeat this until your Miniature American Shepherd lifts its paw to touch the bottle. Holding the bottle just slightly out and down a bit will encourage your Miniature American Shepherd to use its paw. Treat your Miniature American Shepherd when it touches the bottle with its paw.

3. Tap the bottle on the inside of your Miniature American Shepherd's leg when it raises its paw, then press the bottle against your Miniature American Shepherd's chest. Say 'Grip'.

You should still keep your hand on the bottle at this point to prevent your Miniature American Shepherd simply dropping it. You will undoubtedly have to repeat this step several times until your Miniature American Shepherd understands to hold the bottle against its chest.

4. The next step will involve removing your hand from the bottle once your Miniature American Shepherd has taken it. If your Miniature American Shepherd drops the bottle initially, just persevere and the length of time your Miniature American Shepherd holds the bottle will improve.

5. You can now start introducing other objects, presenting them with the command 'Grip'. As long as the object is given in the same manner and with the same word of command, it shouldn't be too difficult for your Miniature American Shepherd to grip any object with which you present it.

Advanced Trick 6

Skateboarding

If you have seen any videos of dogs skateboarding, it's not hard to see how much fun they are having. Before starting skateboarding, be sure to use a good sized board for your Miniature American Shepherd, in accordance with its age/size.

You can start to teach this trick in your home, and a carpeted surface can make it easier for your Miniature American Shepherd to get started as it provides for some traction. If you teach this outside, make sure you choose a level surface; a flat area of lawn is fine, too, since the grass will keep the skateboard from moving too quickly. Your Miniature American Shepherd may be somewhat skittish about the skateboard at first so take instructions slowly if necessary and don't be stingy with praise and treats for every little success. You will be using the verbal cue 'Skate' or 'Ride', whichever you are more comfortable with.

1. Put the skateboard on the floor or ground in front of your Miniature American Shepherd. As soon as your Miniature American Shepherd looks at the skateboard, praise it and give it a treat. At this point, you want your Miniature American Shepherd to associate the skateboard with something pleasant.

2. The next step is to get your Miniature American Shepherd to touch the skateboard. To begin with, even if your Miniature American Shepherd uses its nose, reward it. You might want to hold the board still to prevent your Miniature American Shepherd from becoming startled if it moves. You can even put a treat onto the skateboard to stimulate interest.

3. Reward your Miniature American Shepherd as soon as its foot is planted on the skateboard. Still holding the skateboard still, encourage your Miniature American Shepherd to put both front paws onto the board. If you have taught your Miniature American Shepherd the 'Stack' command, this step will be all the easier.

4. Hold the board steady with your foot and get your Miniature American Shepherd to come closer to your hand. This will serve to draw the hind feet up onto the skateboard. You can keep one hand on your Miniature American Shepherd at this point to help it feel secure.

5. Get your Miniature American Shepherd off and onto the skateboard several times until it does this without hesitation. You can allow the board to move a few inches now to accustom your Miniature American Shepherd to the movement.

6. The next time you get your Miniature American Shepherd ready to get onto the skateboard, say 'Skate' (or 'Ride').

7. Now it's time to get moving. You can keep your hand on your Miniature American Shepherd's back to help it get started by pushing it forward slowly. Take your hand off your Miniature American Shepherd and go in front of it, holding out a treat.

8. Your Miniature American Shepherd may just jump off the skateboard to get the treat, but in this case do not give it. Repeat the 'Skate' command to get your Miniature American Shepherd back up onto the skateboard. Your Miniature American Shepherd will soon learn that getting off the board does not result in a treat and praise and will start using its legs to propel itself.

9. Let your Miniature American Shepherd decide how it is most comfortable when pushing; in some cases, your Miniature American Shepherd will use only the hind legs, or it will use front and back on one side, or only one of the hind legs – it doesn't matter, it only matters that your Miniature American Shepherd is moving.

10. Note: Some of our dogs have become so good at skateboarding that they can use the transition terrain available at skateparks.

Advanced Trick 7

Put Toys Away

A full day of play usually means that your Miniature American Shepherd's toys are scattered all over the home. If you're tired of picking up after your Miniature American Shepherd, you can teach it to put its toys away when it's time for bed. You will have to have a chest or basket large enough to hold all the toys (a cardboard box is fine, too).

1. Put one of your Miniature American Shepherd's toys on the floor near you, point to the toy, and tell your Miniature American Shepherd to 'Fetch'.

2. As soon as your Miniature American Shepherd approaches you, present the basket or box and tell your Miniature American Shepherd 'Drop'.

3. Chances are that the toy will land on the floor next to the basket to begin with. In this case, take a step or two back, point to the toy, and tell your Miniature American Shepherd to 'Fetch'.

When your Miniature American Shepherd brings the toy, hold out the basket again and say 'Drop'.

4. Once your Miniature American Shepherd understands that the toy is supposed to be dropped into the basket, you can start using the phrase 'Put Toys Away'.

5. Begin with 'Fetch' while pointing to a toy, then add in the target phrase. Repeating this step with all your Miniature American Shepherd's toys will help your Miniature American Shepherd to understand that all the toys must be brought to the basket or box. Make sure you take advantage of toys that are in another room so that your Miniature American Shepherd realizes that even toys that cannot be seen are subject to the trick.

6. As soon as your Miniature American Shepherd has the toy over the basket, say 'Drop'. Hold the basket beneath your Miniature American Shepherd's mouth to begin with to make it easier for the trick to be understood. If your Miniature American Shepherd misses the basket, put the toy into your Miniature American Shepherd's mouth, hold the basket beneath your Miniature American Shepherd's mouth and tell your Miniature American Shepherd 'Drop'. After several repetitions you can put the basket on the floor.

7. Now that your Miniature American Shepherd understands how to 'Fetch' the toys and 'Drop' them in the basket, use the phrase 'Put Toys Away' consistently. You will probably have to use 'Fetch' and 'Drop' as initial cues for a while, though.

Advanced Trick 8

Walk on Front Legs

Before you attempt to teach your Miniature American Shepherd this trick, it is imperative that you visit your veterinarian to be sure that your Miniature American Shepherd is physically up to it. This should not be taught to any Miniature American Shepherd under 1 year of age, and any Miniature American Shepherds that are having joint problems of any kind should not do this.

This trick will take a while to perfect simply because your Miniature American Shepherd has to learn to use and build up a different set of muscles. Our Miniature American Shepherd had a very large head and shoulders and if he tried to go downstairs the regular way, he would fall. On his own, he learned to lift his hind legs up over his head and go down the stairs on his front feet. He never fell once doing this and had perfect balance. It was a startling sight the first time we saw it.

You won't need a lot of equipment, just a bunch of books and other household items. Once again, be sure to ask your vet if your Miniature American Shepherd is at the right stage and physically ready for this trick.

1. The first step involves getting your Miniature American Shepherd used to having its hind legs elevated. You can do this by placing a book on the floor under your Miniature American Shepherd, then using a treat to get your Miniature American Shepherd to move forward until the back feet are resting on the book. If all else fails, just put the book under your Miniature American Shepherd's feet.

2. Use one book until your Miniature American Shepherd is comfortable with this degree of elevation and steps onto the book without resistance.

3. It's time now to get your Miniature American Shepherd to step backwards onto the book. You can do this by pushing a treat at your Miniature American Shepherd to encourage its backward movement. If your Miniature American Shepherd is moving all over the place, box your Miniature American Shepherd in using furniture so that it has no choice than to back up onto the book. Use the phrase 'Back Up'.

4. You should gradually increase the number of books used, but should add no more than 1 book a week. This will give your Miniature American Shepherd's muscles time to adjust and strengthen. As the pile grows, move it until it is resting against a wall, this will help to keep it steady.

5. The number of books you use will be dependent upon the overall size and stage of your Miniature American Shepherd. Obviously a smaller Miniature American Shepherd won't require the use of a column of books.

6. Once you have reached a height where your Miniature American Shepherd's hind legs are over its head, remove the books and use the wall only. As your Miniature American Shepherd backs up to the wall, it will probably scramble with its hind legs. Don't be surprised if you have to let your Miniature American Shepherd use the books again several times until it's comfortable with the wall.

7. The aim now is to get your Miniature American Shepherd to abandon the wall and books and put its hind feet into the air. Every time your Miniature American Shepherd gets its feet off the ground, even for a second, treat and praise. Now use the word 'Up'.

8. This trick will take quite a bit of time to teach successfully, so will require a lot of patience on your part.

9. When your Miniature American Shepherd is steady just standing on its front feet you can encourage it to walk by holding a treat in front of its nose and pulling slowly away from your Miniature American Shepherd.

Hopefully, all has gone well with teaching your Miniature American Shepherd tricks, and both of you have progressed through easy to difficult ones without too many problems. If you have used positive reinforcement to teach your Miniature

American Shepherd, both of you are probably much closer than you were before you began.

Chapter Eight: Mission Impossible?

It is true that literally any Miniature American Shepherd can be taught tricks of some kind, but if you have been struggling with yours, there could be a number of factors that are preventing your Miniature American Shepherd from learning any kind of trick. Like within any breed, some are more receptive to learning tricks, while others may be more independent or stubborn.

Stubbornness

It is quite true that some Miniature American Shepherds can simply be stubborn and resist learning tricks. Our 3 puppies were able to learn the basic obedience commands after only a few repetitions, but after showing us that they had learned them, they have steadfastly refused to obey since. If we say 'Come', they will sit down, and if we say 'Sit', they will turn their backs on us. This was never a big issue with us, so we have never bothered again to try to teach them, but those of you with stubborn Miniature American Shepherds will have to work harder to find what motivates your Miniature American Shepherd and use that to teach it tricks.

Impatience

Yes, working with a stubborn Miniature American Shepherd can be frustrating, but dogs in general are very sensitive to our moods and can pick up on negative feelings. Becoming impatient with your Miniature American Shepherd makes it more likely that you will yell at it or even hit it. Keep in mind that when you are training your Miniature American Shepherd, you are also training yourself. Keeping training sessions short will not only keep your Miniature American Shepherd interested, it will also help you remain patient and positive. The owner becoming impatient with the speed at which your Miniature American Shepherd is learning is probably the biggest reason for failure.

Physical Problems

If you have been having trouble teaching your Miniature American Shepherd tricks, the problem might lie in your Miniature American Shepherd's body. Your Miniature American Shepherd just might not be able to jump high, for instance, or it could be that it is harboring some type of longstanding fear.

There could also be a medical reason why your adult or puppy Miniature American Shepherd is not responding as you would wish; Miniature American Shepherds with hip dysplasia will find it impossible to do most tricks. Miniature American Shepherds that have arthritis will also be reluctant to get involved in tricks. If you have any question about your Miniature American Shepherd's physical ability to do tricks, speak to your veterinarian.

Infections can also impact your Miniature American Shepherd's receptivity to instructions, making it less likely to pay attention to you because it is uncomfortable. There could also be hearing issues that are affecting your Miniature American Shepherd's ability to learn tricks – if the latter turns out to be the case, use hand signals.

Mental Slowness

Yes, it's true, some Miniature American Shepherds are just mentally slow. This does not mean that they cannot be taught tricks at all, it does mean that they probably will not be able to learn without very many repetitions, and that you will have to have enormous patience to teach them. You will find geniuses and 'dummies' in every breed, but this will not affect your Miniature American Shepherd's capacity for affection. If you do find that for whatever reason, your Miniature American Shepherd is unable or unwilling to become a star, accept your Miniature American Shepherd as it is, and just enjoy life together.

Chapter Nine: Games for Both of You

If you've been thinking that tricks are a bit one-sided, with your Miniature American Shepherd doing all the activity at your verbal command or physical signal, you'll undoubtedly love to engage in games with your Miniature American Shepherd. Teaching tricks has been a good way for you to work together towards a goal, and will be the foundation of not only doing games together, but also for agility if you are so inclined.

Games will involve activities in which you are both participating, rather than you simply giving commands that your Miniature American Shepherd must obey. When your Miniature American Shepherd is carrying out tricks, it is performing for you, when you are playing games with your Miniature American Shepherd, you are both acting as a team. Some of these games are good for indoors and are great when the weather is so wet, cold, or hot that you don't want to be outside, while others are perfect for the outdoors, and some can be played anywhere.

Also, keep in mind that like any other breed, Miniature American Shepherds need both mental and physical stimulation to stay healthy. Many of the problems that arise with Miniature American Shepherds, such as nuisance barking, aggression, or destructive behavior, come about because your Miniature American Shepherd had no outlet for its energy and simply has become bored. Games with your Miniature American Shepherd will be more fun for both of you if you vary them and keep play sessions fairly short.

As with any activity in which you engage with your Miniature American Shepherd, there are some rules for you to follow in order to have the games safe: try to avoid vigorous outdoor games when the weather is hot. There have been some cases of heat stroke.

Make certain that your adult or puppy Miniature American Shepherd does not have any health problems that could adversely affect it while playing games. Older dogs, too, will probably appreciate shorter, less rigorous game sessions so that they do not get tired out or injure themselves.

Also, if your pup grew up quickly then it should be monitored carefully when engaging in very physical games with them – a fast rate of growth can leave joints somewhat vulnerable to damage.

The Tissue Game

Many years ago, I had a Miniature American Shepherd that was just crazy about this game. We used a piece of ordinary facial tissue, but a small toy or even a little piece of cloth is just as good. This game is played with you sitting in a chair or on the sofa and using the lure to flash between and around your legs. My Miniature American Shepherd would often indicate that she was ready to play the tissue game by coming over and butting her head against my legs. One of the nicest things about the Tissue Game is that there is absolutely no previous training needed for playing it.

1. Wiggle the lure to get your Miniature American Shepherd's attention. If your Miniature American Shepherd doesn't seem to get it, touch your Miniature American Shepherd's nose with the lure and say 'Get it!' in an enthusiastic tone. If tissue is being shredded, or attempted to be eaten by your pooch, use a cloth or a small toy.

2. Move the lure from between the middle of your legs to one side or another and watch your Miniature American Shepherd dart around happily after it. This is a good game for inclement weather days.

Chase

You can make a lure for your Miniature American Shepherd by tying one end of a 2 foot piece of string to a scrap of cloth or a small toy and tying the other end to a stick, or even use a long grass stem with the seed head attached (our puppies just loved this one).

1. After you have prepared the lure, put it on the floor or ground in front of your pup.

2. Wiggle it around a bit to get your Miniature American Shepherd's interest then start pulling it away. Your Miniature American Shepherd's prey drive will probably kick in right away.

3. Most Miniature American Shepherd adults and puppies will start chasing the lure without any encouragement from you.

4. If your Miniature American Shepherd refuses to chase the lure, you can substitute a treat such as a doggie biscuit to challenge their interest.

5. This is a good way to give your Miniature American Shepherd some exercise indoors when the weather is keeping you inside.

Hide and Seek

This game can be played inside or out and makes use not only of your Miniature American Shepherd's desire to be with you, but also of the prey drive that all Miniature American Shepherds possess. If you do play this outside, play it in a fenced yard so that your Miniature American Shepherd doesn't wander off while you're hiding. Most Miniature American Shepherds quickly learn the names of the humans in the household, making your Miniature American Shepherd's participation even easier. Generally speaking, this game is easier with two humans.

1. To begin this game, put your Miniature American Shepherd into 'Stay'.

2. Go to the opposite side of the room and crouch down behind a piece of furniture.

3. Once you are hidden, the human helper should tell your Miniature American Shepherd 'Find Papa (or Mama, or Tommy, or whoever)'.

4. As soon as your Miniature American Shepherd locates the hidden person, give your Miniature American Shepherd a treat and praise it.

5. Your Miniature American Shepherd will probably catch on to how to play this quickly and you can extend the search area to adjoining rooms, or anywhere in the house or yard. You can probably start to give treats only now and again, but keep up with the praise.

Bubbles

This should be done outside unless you want soap residue on your furniture and carpeting. Purchase non-toxic bubble solution so that it won't hurt your Miniature American Shepherd if it does happen to get into its eyes or mouth. In fact, pet stores sell bubble solutions that smell and taste like meat, which should make this game even easier for your Miniature American Shepherd to learn. Start this on a calm day, then wait for a breezy one to really have some fun with your Miniature American Shepherd as it chases after the fleeing bubbles.

1. Sit down so that you are on the same level as your Miniature American Shepherd and call your Miniature American Shepherd to you.

2. When you have your Miniature American Shepherd's attention, blow out a bubble.

3. Curiosity will often spur your Miniature American Shepherd to touch its nose to the bubble.

4. If your Miniature American Shepherd doesn't seem interested, or doesn't seem to know what to do, you can put your own nose near the bubble to give your Miniature American Shepherd the idea.

5. Dogs love to chase things, and most Miniature American Shepherds, once they see a bubble floating past them will go right after it.

Let's Dance!

Your Miniature American Shepherd will have to know how to stand on its hind legs reliably before you can start to teach it to dance. Because this can put a strain on it, make certain that your vet checks out your Miniature American Shepherd, especially the hips and back, before you start teaching your Miniature American Shepherd to trip the light fantastic. When beginning 'Let's Dance', definitely keep the sessions short, particularly if your Miniature American Shepherd hasn't done too much work standing up. Do not try to teach your Miniature American Shepherd to dance unless it has already been through obedience training and at least the intermediate tricks; the more your Miniature American Shepherd is used to working with you, the easier it will be to teach dancing.

1. Tell your Miniature American Shepherd 'Stand Up'. Praise and treat.

2. To get your Miniature American Shepherd to wave its front paws around, hold a treat above its nose. Use a hand signal, such as a waving motion with your right hand to familiarize your Miniature American Shepherd with this phase of the lesson.

3. When you want your Miniature American Shepherd to move towards you on its hind legs, back away from it while holding a treat up above its nose. Make a beckoning motion with your hand now.

4. To get your Miniature American Shepherd to walk backwards, move towards your Miniature American Shepherd, holding the treat above the nose as before. Put your palm towards your Miniature American Shepherd to signal backing up.

5. Always remember to treat and praise at every small positive step.

6. If you want your Miniature American Shepherd to twirl around, circle the treat over your Miniature American Shepherd's head. Make a twirling motion with one hand.

7. Keep practicing with your Miniature American Shepherd these basic steps, adding music to let your Miniature American Shepherd associate the rhythm of the piece you have chosen with its dance movements. Now you can add 'Let's Dance' to your Miniature American Shepherd's vocabulary.

8. As you and your Miniature American Shepherd become more adept as a dance team, you can add some more complicated moves such as pirouetting under your arm while you hold one of your Miniature American Shepherd's paws, or dipping down then rising up again.

9. Stick to one fairly short musical selection at first and repeat the same steps as you play it; you are actually now the choreographer. Soon your Miniature American Shepherd won't even need hand signals or treats during the performance, but will take its cues from the music and your dance movements.

You can definitely add other pieces of music once your Miniature American Shepherd has learned the first, but be sure that you only add one at a time, and your Miniature American Shepherd should be proficient and confident in each piece before you add another one.

Ball Roll & Toss

This will be best as a game involving 2 people along with your Miniature American Shepherd. Several dogs can also play this as long as you're certain they won't fight. The best kind of ball to use for this is the 'clutch ball' type which is a sculpted ball with indentations that facilitate your Miniature American Shepherd being able to pick up a fairly large ball in its mouth.

1. Position yourself at least 15 feet away from the other person.

2. Show the ball to your Miniature American Shepherd and then toss it to the other person. Hopefully, your Miniature American Shepherd will run in that direction.

3. If your Miniature American Shepherd doesn't seem to catch on, roll the ball, that should definitely get your Miniature American Shepherd's prey drive activated.

4. Once your Miniature American Shepherd starts to play, this can give everyone involved a real workout.

5. When interest begins to flag, let your Miniature American Shepherd 'catch' the ball and chase it to make the end of the game more engaging for your Miniature American Shepherd.

Water Fun

Nothing can help you and your Miniature American Shepherd cool off on a hot summer day than playing in the water. You can use a beach, a lake, a pool (even a kiddie pool), or even a hose to have fun with water. Do not hesitate to equip your Miniature American Shepherd with a personal floatation device (PFD).

1. The hose can be a great source of cooling fun for you and your Miniature American Shepherd. You can either use the hose on a wide angle spray to give your Miniature American Shepherd a dose of water, or you can set up the sprinkler to let both of you

get wet. Most Miniature American Shepherds love this, but if yours does not, don't force it and find some other way to cool off.

2. A backyard pool can not only help you and your Miniature American Shepherd shed some excess body heat, but it's also a good place to play with a ball or other floating toy. One caution is to not let your Miniature American Shepherd swallow the water as it could get water drunk and require veterinary care. If all you have is a kiddie pool, most Miniature American Shepherds will be just as happy splashing around with you or the kids.

3. Lakes can give you and your Miniature American Shepherd chances to swim and play together. Playing with a ball in a lake gives you both more space for your game. You can also play water tag with your Miniature American Shepherd. As with a backyard pool, don't let your Miniature American Shepherd drink the lake water.

4. If online videos are any indication, there is hardly a dog alive that doesn't love playing games at the beach. You can run races with your Miniature American Shepherd and chase one another through the surf. Don't forget to bring a ball along, too, to throw into the surf for your Miniature American Shepherd to paddle out to.

Surfing

If you love surfing and would love for your Miniature American Shepherd to enjoy it too, there is no reason why your Miniature American Shepherd cannot learn to ride the board with you. The first prerequisite is that your Miniature American Shepherd has no fear of the water and swims well. A doggy 'life preserver' is also a necessity, and you should choose one that will hold your Miniature American Shepherd's head above the water. Many dog PFDs have handles on the back that will make it easy to pull your Miniature American Shepherd out of the water if it has slipped off the board.

You can have your Miniature American Shepherd surf right on your board with you, or your Miniature American Shepherd can surf on its own board; you and your Miniature American Shepherd will have to decide what works best for the both of you. A longboard will be needed if you are both going to share a board, and a shortboard if your Miniature American Shepherd is going to surf on its own (you will still need to push your Miniature American Shepherd out past the breakers if it's using a shortboard).

1. Your choice of surfboard will be important – you will need one that has a hard surface so as not to harm your Miniature American Shepherd's foot pads – foam boards can damage the skin on your Miniature American Shepherd's feet. You will also want a board that provides good traction.

2. Introducing your Miniature American Shepherd to the surfboard can be done by letting your Miniature American Shepherd become familiar with the board while it's on the floor or the ground. Let your Miniature American Shepherd sniff at the board and encourage it to get onto the board. You can even just put your Miniature American Shepherd on the board, praising and treating when it is on it.

3. If your Miniature American Shepherd balks at getting on even a board sitting on your living room floor, place treats on the board to help your Miniature American Shepherd overcome its apprehension.

4. Once your Miniature American Shepherd is comfortable sitting or lying on the board on the floor or ground, you can take it to the next step – the ocean. (If your Miniature American Shepherd is skittish, you can use some friends to lift the board and carry it on the beach just to get your Miniature American Shepherd used to the unfamiliar motion.)

5. Choose a calm day to introduce your Miniature American Shepherd to sitting on the surfboard in the water. Keep the board close to shore and place your Miniature American Shepherd onto it. Some Miniature American Shepherds seem to have a surfing gene and will take to the board immediately, others will need some help.

6. Get onto the rear portion of the board, sitting or standing, and paddle around a bit to get your Miniature American Shepherd accustomed to motion. If your Miniature American Shepherd jumps off, just start over again, but never betray any impatience or disappointment.

7. Small waves are the next step in canine surfing, only between 1 and 2 feet. Keep in mind that solo canine surfers will only be able to handle waves twice that height, if you want your Miniature American Shepherd to catch the big ones, the two of you will have to share a board.

8. You will always have to shred for your Miniature American Shepherd if it has its own board.

9. There will always be the odd Miniature American Shepherd that takes to surfing like a dolphin to the water, but most Miniature American Shepherds will require many repetitions before they are adept and comfortable at it.

Frisbee (Disc) Toss

Have you always been envious of those dogs that chase after a Frisbee when it's flying through the air and catch it effortlessly in their mouths? This a game that you and your Miniature American Shepherd can really enjoy together, although it could take quite a bit of practice. Make sure you have a Miniature American Shepherd that is physically able to play this game as it will require quite a bit of energy and bounce.

1. Don't buy a 'cheapie' Frisbee or disc, these are usually hard plastic and can hurt your Miniature American Shepherd's mouth when taken on the fly. There are discs available made of rubber or soft plastic that will be kinder to your Miniature American Shepherd's teeth, lips, and tongue.

2. It's often a good idea to start out with a floppy disc which is easier for the novice disc chaser to handle. You can move on to more rigid ones once your Miniature American Shepherd has gotten used to the game and understands how best to catch the disc.

3. If your Miniature American Shepherd ignores or even seems apprehensive of the disc, you can get your Miniature American Shepherd to like the disc by placing it on the ground and putting some treats on it. This will also help to associate treats with the disc in your Miniature American Shepherd's mind.

4. Throw the disc a short distance away and give your Miniature American Shepherd the 'Fetch' command. Treat, praise, and repeat. Your Miniature American Shepherd will probably just drop the disc at your feet on its own, but if it retains it in its mouth, tell your Miniature American Shepherd to 'Drop' and it should let go of the disc.

5. Making the leap from retrieving the disc to catching it in the air is the difficult part. It can be made a bit easier if you roll the disc on its edge for your Miniature American Shepherd to chase. This will get your Miniature American Shepherd used to snatching at the rim of the disc while it's moving.

6. When your Miniature American Shepherd is plucking up the rolling disc without problem, you can take the game to the next step – throwing the disc into the air.

7. Make your first throws short, only a couple of feet and encourage your Miniature American Shepherd by saying 'Fetch'. Don't be disappointed if it takes some time for your Miniature

American Shepherd to get the hang of this, the agility level of your Miniature American Shepherd will be important here.

8. Extend the length of the throws and be sure to treat and praise every time your Miniature American Shepherd manages to grab the disc. Generally with a bit of practice, most Miniature American Shepherds will begin to leap at the disc as it flies through the air. This is great exercise for your Miniature American Shepherd, especially.

Obstacle Course

You can construct an obstacle course either inside and/or outside for your Miniature American Shepherd. Although this might be a great way to 'break in' your Miniature American Shepherd for future agility work, it's fun to do for both of you just on its own. Using household items is an easy way to give your Miniature American Shepherd some physical and mental challenges.

1. Kitchen and dining room chairs can be used to form a tunnel for your Miniature American Shepherd to run through, especially if you drape the sides with blankets. You can encourage your Miniature American Shepherd to run down the tunnel either by throwing a treat or toy down it or getting at the opposite end of the tunnel and calling your Miniature American Shepherd.

2. Jumps can be created indoors as easily as piling up two stacks of books and laying a yardstick across them.

3. You can make an indoor weave course for your Miniature American Shepherd by lining up objects such as pails, vinyl winter boots, and empty drawers set on end. To really get into the spirit of play with your Miniature American Shepherd, you can lead it through the weave course yourself.

4. Hard-seated chairs can also be fastened together to make an elevated run for your Miniature American Shepherd. You will have to make sure that the chair won't separate when your

Miniature American Shepherd is on them – use bungee cords. Unless you will have your Miniature American Shepherd jump up onto the chair, use a ramp or doggy stairs to get your Miniature American Shepherd up.

5. If you don't mind a bit of noise and controlled mayhem, build a tower out of empty cans and let your Miniature American Shepherd knock it over. You can make this a reward, if you like, for successfully traversing a tunnel or managing a jump.

Chapter Ten: Play is Therapeutic

All of us have heard the old expression "All work and no play makes Jack a dull boy", and this is relevant not only for people but also for Miniature American Shepherds. Never let teaching tricks to your Miniature American Shepherd become work to either of you, but always keep the training sessions short and positive. Playing and interacting with your Miniature American Shepherd is not only a good way to bond more closely with your Miniature American Shepherd, but it will also have some health benefits for you, and for your Miniature American Shepherd.

Weight

If you and your Miniature American Shepherd have found yourselves becoming a bit pudgy, instituting a regular program of tricks and games can help both of you get back into shape (if you keep your Miniature American Shepherd treats small, of course). Some of the more active games you will be playing with your Miniature American Shepherd such as swimming, surfing, dancing, and chasing will keep your muscles toned and your bodies fit. As your Miniature American Shepherd ages, play and tricks will help to keep your Miniature American Shepherd's joints strong. Keeping excess weight off also helps with your Miniature American Shepherd's heart health.

Stress

Stress will most likely pertain to you. It's no secret how hectic most of our lives are and stress can have some very negative effects on us such as damaging our hearts, elevating our blood pressure, and causing nervous disorders. Insomnia is another negative effect of stress, and people (and probably dogs) who are stressed are more likely to become ill as their immune systems take a beating from stress hormones.

Teaching tricks to your Miniature American Shepherd and engaging in games with it will help you to relax and unwind after a hard day. The unconditional love your Miniature American Shepherd has for you will also help to reduce your stress levels. It has been found that people who share their lives with dogs tend to live longer lives than those who do not. Interacting with a dog can keep blood pressure at a reasonable level and even lower high blood pressure.

Behavior

If you have ever come home and found the house torn apart and perhaps marked with undesirable substances (poop and pee), your Miniature American Shepherd is probably very bored and frustrated. Miniature American Shepherds are intelligent and when they have no mental or physical stimulation, they will become bored and find some way to alleviate it, usually be engaging in a destructive behavior of some kind. Nuisance barking, aggression to people and other pets, as well as the ability to destroy property generally all stem in boredom. Not only can all Miniature American Shepherds destroy upholstered furniture and apparel, some could even actually damage the physical structure of the home.

Don't let all the tricks and games presented in this guide overwhelm you, proceed at the pace that works best for you and your Miniature American Shepherd, you're not in a race. You and your Miniature American Shepherd are not obligated to do any specific number of them, the choice is up to you. The object of teaching your Miniature American Shepherd tricks is to have fun, as well as provide your Miniature American Shepherd with some mental and physical stimulation.

Chapter Eleven: Agility – The Ultimate in Games

Have you ever been fascinated watching the talented dogs perform agility feats and wondered whether your Miniature American Shepherd might do well with this? Well, you certainly aren't alone as can be seen by the popularity of agility in so many countries. Considering how many people and dogs are engaged in agility, it might surprise you to learn that it's a relative newcomer on the dog scene.

It all started as a way to keep the audience at the Crufts Dog Show in England from becoming bored while waiting for the next event to start. One of the event organizers, John Varley, can be credited with the idea. Basing the activities of your Miniature American Shepherds on the stunts performed by horses at horse shows, agility was found to be an excellent way to keep the crowd engaged during any hiatus, and it was an instant hit with the audience.

However, the few simple routines initially offered proved to be so overwhelmingly popular that agility now has become one of the favorite activities of dogs and their owners. Shortly after its first introduction, dog owners were demanding classes and events for agility.

It is still a real pleaser when it comes to audiences at dog shows, too, even for those who are not actively engaged in agility with their dog. Agility trials are offered on both an amateur and professional level, and agility can now be considered a very competitive sport. Considering how much a part of your dog world agility now is, it's hard to believe that it only started up in 1978.

Agility is basically an obstacle course laid out for your Miniature American Shepherd to navigate with your assistance. If agility looks like something you might want to become involved in with your Miniature American Shepherd, make sure that your Miniature American Shepherd has 'graduated' from obedience training and is properly socialized.

For those of you who have skipped obedience training, please see our previous book: Miniature American Shepherd Training Guide, for detailed instructions. Likewise, Miniature American Shepherds that have not been socialized will need to be; for those of you who are really becoming involved past the backyard level of agility, it is imperative that your Miniature American Shepherd has the ability to either get along with other dogs or ignore them completely. Any dog acting aggressively towards another at a competition will be eliminated from the trials out of hand.

For those of you who have been teaching tricks and engaging in games with your Miniature American Shepherd, agility could easily be considered the next step up. And, if your Miniature American Shepherd has already been playing with you using a simple obstacle course as mentioned earlier, then the groundwork has already been laid. Clicker training will certainly come in handy here, if you have been training your Miniature American Shepherd with a clicker, but if whatever method you have been using has been successful, then don't hesitate to keep using it – it's never wise to argue with success.

Agility trials will consist of a course that contains between 12 and 18 obstacles. Some of the obstacles, particularly the jumps, will often be repeated over the length of the course. You should keep in mind that there is no set pattern to the obstacles and the set-up will vary from competition to competition.

Prior to beginning the trial, owners and their dogs will have a chance to have a dry run to familiarize themselves with the course, and at this point it's probably better to take your Miniature American Shepherd through it on leash. The differing arrangements at the competitions is why it's a good idea to alter the plan of your own obstacle course from time to time so that your Miniature American Shepherd becomes used to varied course arrangements.

Consider Your Miniature American Shepherd

Theoretically, any Miniature American Shepherd, can participate in agility, but there are still some factors that should be taken into consideration before you begin.

1. The health of your Miniature American Shepherd is the first consideration. Agility is a very demanding sport, and in order for your Miniature American Shepherd to do well in it, and reduce the chance that it will be injured, it should be in top physical condition. A complete checkup at the veterinarian is certainly called for, including blood work. Your Miniature American Shepherd's hips should be free from any degenerative disease or malformation. The spine should be in perfect condition; x-rays can detect any small compression fractures of other problems, and if your Miniature American Shepherd has a family history of hip dysplasia, then additionally have your vet x-ray the hips.

2. The shape and weight of your Miniature American Shepherd will make a difference in how much it is able to accomplish in agility. Heavier Miniature American Shepherds can have a hard time, although there has been success in a variety of cases and so given the correct training and routine, things can work out for you.

3. Make an honest assessment of your Miniature American Shepherd's potential, especially if you are contemplating

competitions at a higher level. If you are just going to do agility for fun, then potential will make little or no difference.

4. The age of your Miniature American Shepherd is also important; dogs too young or too old are not good candidates for the intensive demands of agility work. Trials or meets will have age limitations on all dogs.

5. Hyperactive dogs can actually be a good choice for agility. If you have a Miniature American Shepherd that seems to be constantly bouncing off the walls, maybe it's time to channel all that canine energy into something constructive, like agility. Because owners sometimes give up on a hyper dog, you may have to go back and work on obedience first. However, both obedience and agility can provide an outlet for your Miniature American Shepherd's high energy level. With this type of dog, an extra dose of patience on your part will probably be needed, but you may well be surprised at how well your Miniature American Shepherd does do with agility once it gets used to it – and you may have a Miniature American Shepherd that is now calmer and more pleasant to be around. Giving a hyper Miniature American Shepherd something to do is often the best way to cure this problem behavior, and it's certainly better than consigning it to a shelter.

Chapter Twelve: Pre-Agility for Puppies

Important Points

If you think agility looks like something that would be fun for you and your new puppy, there are some things to consider before you leap into the sport.

1. As it is with human children, and with the young of all species with backbones, the growth plates of the bones of puppies are still open. The growth plate is also known as the epiphyseal plate and is responsible for the production of cells that will wind up as actual bone tissue. You can picture your puppy's leg bones as consisting of a middle length of cartilage capped at either end by growth plates. The growth plates are constantly producing new cells which are continuously being pushed toward the center of the leg. As these cells migrate, they begin to ossify, turn to bone, replacing the cartilage. Eventually, the cartilage is all replaced and the place where the cells from both plates finally meet is called the epiphyseal line. Until the growth plates have completed their work, there is always a chance that serious harm could be done to the leg. Puppies that are over-exercised or encouraged to jump or run too much could wind up with damaged, stunted legs and a permanent limp.

2. The joints of puppies can also be damaged by too much physical activity. Between the bones of a dog's joint is cartilage, which provides cushioning so that the bones don't grind together. Jumping too much, and even running too much, can cause the cartilage to become damaged. Arthritis and/or hip dysplasia can result. A limping dog will not be allowed in any agility competition, so go easy on those joints while your Miniature American Shepherd is young.

3. Do not, under any circumstances, use a weighted vest on your Miniature American Shepherd puppy to attempt to build up more muscle; you will only be increasing the probability of damage to the growth plates or joints. These vests could also affect your puppy's balance, making it more likely that the puppy will fall and hurt itself.

4. Avoid using weave poles when starting puppy agility – these can cause torsion, or spiral, fractures to the pup's undeveloped leg bones. A spiral fracture can also occur if the puppy jumps from a high spot. Unlike a 'normal' fracture which is usually a break along the horizontal in the leg, a torsion fracture spirals up the bone. You might consider that in this case the puppy's leg has essentially been twisted apart. Unlike a simple fracture, which is relatively easy to treat, a torsion fracture will require surgery and your vet will probably have to use pins to keep the pieces of the bone together. Most dogs will limp permanently after receiving a spiral fracture, regardless of aftercare.

Easy Does It

If you can't wait to get started on pre-agility training with your Miniature American Shepherd puppy, you should wait until it is at least 4 months old. This is not only a good time for teaching your puppy new skills, but also a window for bonding with you. However, you must keep the activities at a much lower level than you would than if you were working with an adult Miniature American Shepherd.

Keep in mind that reputable agility competitions will not allow a dog to compete until it is 12 months old, and even older for some trials and breeds. Large and giant breed should definitely be kept from performing the higher jumps until they are about 18 months old as their greater weight puts much more stress on the bones and joints that will be experienced by a smaller and lighter puppy.

Never forget that your puppy is just that – a puppy, even when it looks as if it has attained its full growth. Not only will your puppy's attention span be short, but it will also be full of nearly boundless energy, and this is exactly where you will have to exhibit restraint during training; your puppy may want to do more than is good for it. Even if your puppy takes to pre-agility readily and eagerly, you will have to limit training sessions to make sure that too much exercise does not harm the pup.

Pre-agility is a great time to accustom your Miniature American Shepherd puppy to hand signals as well as verbal instruction. Use both when working out with the puppy and you will soon be able to use them interchangeably. Always treat for even the smallest success and completely ignore any slip-up. Never push your puppy to keep trying an obstacle or lesson that is giving problems, this will only activate your puppy's stubborn streak and you will not only find it harder to teach this particular lesson, but others as well. A character in a book once said, "Never give an order unless you're sure it will be obeyed", and these are words of wisdom, even when pertaining to Miniature American Shepherds.

Introducing your Miniature American Shepherd puppy to the basic obstacles of agility at this stage is a good idea as long as you scale the obstacles to your puppy's age and physical condition. Keeping the obstacles as close to the ground as possible will help familiarize your Miniature American Shepherd puppy with them and make it much less likely that an injury will occur. Some people like to enroll their puppies in puppy agility classes, and this can be not only a good idea as far as agility is concerned, but can also help with socialization. One caveat to always keep in mind if you do use a class is to never allow the instructor to have your puppy do something that you think the puppy is unready for, especially anything involving heights. It's your Miniature American Shepherd, after all. Never hesitate to speak up if you disagree with some part of the instruction or if you think the obstacles are too advanced for your puppy. You have hired the instructor, not the other way around.

Interestingly, it's been found that success not only in agility, but in obedience itself, can be linked to whether or not the owner uses puppy or dog training classes. Those who enroll their pups in a class, but only attend one class, have much less success than people who train the puppy or dog entirely by themselves. However, people who join a class with their companion and stick with it, do achieve faster success than those who train their pooch on their own. Evidently, the message here is that if you are going to undertake something, do it completely – either train your Miniature American Shepherd entirely on your own or enroll in a structured class and follow it to the end.

If you decide to work with your Miniature American Shepherd puppy yourself, you can start preparing it for several of the obstacles simply by placing a board on the ground and letting your pup get used to walking, and then running over it. You can keep your puppy on leash to begin with to prevent it darting off the sides, but can eliminate that as soon as the puppy is used to the board and will navigate it without jumping off one side. Staying on the board will be very important when the board has been elevated several feet off the ground. Some pups may be a bit afraid to get on the board right away, but a line of treats leading to the board and continued on the board itself will usually help any puppy get over its fear.

You can start to accustom your Miniature American Shepherd puppy to traveling through the chute by pushing back the fabric nearly to the start and then encouraging your puppy to go through it. As your pup becomes used to the chute, you can add more fabric until the puppy is able to travel through the entire length without problem. Because it's best for your Miniature American Shepherd to go through both the open and collapsed chutes in agility competitions with its nose down, you can help your pup learn this while familiarizing it with the chute.

1. To encourage your Miniature American Shepherd puppy to keep its nose down, tie a small toy or treat to a length of cord and pull it along in front of the puppy. At this point, keep the chute fabric rolls back so you can see what's going on.

2. Keep praising your pup as it runs along the chute in pursuit of the object with its nose down.

3. Alternate using the lure and just encouraging your puppy through the chute using only verbal cues.

4. Add more and more fabric length to the chute as your Miniature American Shepherd puppy becomes more adept at keeping its nose down.

To help your Miniature American Shepherd puppy with the collapsed chute, start by draping a light weight fabric over the end of the open chute – most puppies will have no problem with just plowing through. To simulate the longer collapsed chute, use a bed sheet to gradually add length to the collapsed part of the chute.

As your puppy progresses and grows older and stronger, you can add more challenges to prepare it for actual agility:

1. A tire sitting upright on the ground, through which the puppy can jump.

2. Jumps using both poles and boards can be introduced, but be sure that they are only an inch or two off the ground to start with; you do not want to take a chance with damaging your puppy's bones or joints.

3. Make a 'pseudo' wobble board, only an inch off the ground, to get the puppy used to the uncertain surface. Don't hesitate to keep your hands on your puppy to help it feel confident; don't be

surprised if your puppy is skittish at first, this is normal and you should be able to overcome it without too much trouble.

4. Likewise, a teeter-totter that tips only an inch or so to start will accustom the pup to the movement of the board. Use the same technique as detailed above to help your pup overcome any fear it has at the movement of the board. Lead your puppy from one side to the other to help it get accustomed to the jar it will feel when the board hits the ground.

Regardless of whether you are teaching your Miniature American Shepherd puppy pre-agility in your own home and backyard or in a class, always remember to go at your puppy's speed. You want your puppy to feel good about learning these maneuvers and to develop the confidence to continue and do well. Never compare your puppy's progress to another puppy in the class, and try to force your pup to 'catch up'. You're not in a competition at this point, so relax and enjoy working with your puppy, you will get much better and longer lasting results if you proceed at your pup's pace.

If you are starting off with a puppy and have children, why not combine them and get your kids involved in agility. This is not an excuse for you to leave the child and the puppy alone to work on the project, but a way for you, your child, and your puppy to all do this together. Children enjoy doing things with their parents, and this can be a great way not only to introduce your kid to dog agility, but also to impart some important lessons about dog care. Be as patient with your child as you would (or should) be with your puppy. Take it slow and easy so that agility is something both young participants look forward to doing. If your youngster really is enthusiastic about this, you might sign him or her up for junior agility classes. Being around other puppies and dogs will help to get your pup used to different situations and people and can also help with socializing your pup.

Chapter Thirteen: Agility Basics for Your Adult Miniature American Shepherd

Now that your puppy has grown up and can be considered to be an adult, it's time to return to the vet for a complete checkup. Explain to your vet that you are interested in agility work with your young adult Miniature American Shepherd and have him or her make sure that your Miniature American Shepherd's hips, legs, and spine are ready to really get going. It's likely that you will get the go-ahead, so you and your Miniature American Shepherd can get down to the fun business of agility. This is also the perfect time to make certain that your Miniature American Shepherd is current on all its shots.

The approach you take to equipment will reflect your agility goals. If you are just planning on doing agility with your Miniature American Shepherd for the fun of it, you can make your own obstacles or use cheaper ones (just make certain they are sturdy enough to prevent injury to your Miniature American Shepherd). However, if you are hoping to take part in judged competitions, you should definitely invest in the highest quality fixtures that you can afford, preferably as close as possible to those that will be used during a competition. This will allow you and your Miniature American Shepherd to become familiar with the obstacles beforehand.

The following are the obstacles used in agility competitions. Your Miniature American Shepherd may already be familiar with these if you have engaged in pre-agility work, but any fit, adult Miniature American Shepherd can also learn how to run the obstacle course as well. If the adult Miniature American Shepherd is coming to these obstacles without any previous experience with them, be sure to introduce your Miniature American Shepherd to them one at a time, and start training slowly. Needless to say, keep a pocketful of treats handy, and do not stint on praise for any small step of progress.

1. **Dog Walk.** This obstacle is made up of 3 boards, 2 of them being used as ramps and the center one horizontal to the ground. Your Miniature American Shepherd is expected to run up one of the ramps, along the horizontal board, then down the opposite board ramp. The horizontal board is 4 feet above the ground. It should be kept in mind that some sponsoring organizations allow traction slats on the ramp boards, while others do not. Some organizations use rubberized boards for traction. If you are serious about agility, it's probably a good idea to get your Miniature American Shepherd used to boards that provide traction and ones that do not.

2. **A-Frame.** The A-Frame is an obstacle that requires your Miniature American Shepherd to climb up one fairly steep ramp, then scramble down the other side on an equally steep ramp. Each ramp is between 8 to 9 feet in length and 3 feet in breadth. The ramps are connected at the top with a hinge. As with the Dog Walk, some organizations allow the use of slats on the ramps to provide footing for your Miniature American Shepherds. Be aware that some competitions will not allow the use of slatted ramps, however. Rubberized A-Frame ramps are allowed, also.

3. **Pause Table.** This is, as it says, a 'table' onto which your Miniature American Shepherd must jump and then either sit or lie for a designated period of time – generally only about 5 seconds. The table is 3 feet square, but can be set at different heights. Some Pause Tables are only 8 inches high, while others are over 2 feet in height (the height will be determined by the height of your Miniature American Shepherd). Besides the Pause Table, some trials will have what is called a Pause Box. This is simply an area on the ground demarcated by tape or perhaps sections of PVC pipe laid on the ground. It would be a good idea to get your Miniature American Shepherd used to this, and use

the same command for the Pause Box and you would for the Pause Table. Remember, the simpler you make things, the greater the chance for success at a trial.

4. **Teeter-Totter**. Based on the children's toy, this is one of the most challenging of obstacles to teach to a Miniature American Shepherd. The abrupt slamming down of the board as your Miniature American Shepherd travels across the midpoint is frightening to most Miniature American Shepherds, at least initially. The midpoint of the Teeter-Totter is several feet above the ground, and one side of the 12 foot board is slightly longer than the other so that the board always descends on that side when not in use. There are no slats or other traction elements on the Teeter-Totter. As can be expected, your Miniature American Shepherd runs up the side of the board on the ground, reaches midpoint, then descends as its weight forces the other side down.

5. **Tunnel**. Made of what is, in effect, a long wire spiral covered with vinyl, and is 10 to 20 feet long. Because of the flexibility of the wire spiral, the tunnel can be straight or positioned into curves. In order to keep the tunnel from moving while your Miniature American Shepherd is traversing it, sandbags are often used to provide stability.

6. **Collapsed Tunnel**. Unlike the regular Tunnel, the Collapsed Tunnel consists of a short stationery arch or a cylinder with a tube of fabric fastened to it, which lies flat on the ground. Your Miniature American Shepherd enters through the arch and must then make its way through the fabric to come out of the other end.

7. **Basic Jump**. Also called the Hurdle, the Basic Jump consists of an obstacle with a horizontal bar that can be adjusted to the height of your Miniature American Shepherd. The bar is supported in place by vertical stanchions. Some jumps have 'wings' to either side of the jump itself, which serve mostly to keep the handler

from getting too close to your Miniature American Shepherd as it goes over the jump.

8. **Panel Jump**. Rather than use bars or poles, this jump uses a solid board instead. As with the Basic Jump, the height of your Miniature American Shepherd will determine the height of the jump.

9. **Spread Jump**. In this jump, which uses horizontal bars, the bars are all aligned on the different levels, and separated from one another to cause your Miniature American Shepherd to traverse not only a vertical plane, but also a horizontal one. The amount of spread, as well as the height, will depend upon the size of your Miniature American Shepherd.

10. **Tire Jump**. Whether an actual tire is used, which has been carefully wrapped with tape to prevent your Miniature American Shepherds' feet from becoming entangled, or a specially designed 'tire', the effect is the same – your Miniature American Shepherd will have to jump through the tire. Suspended in a frame, the height of the tire will be adjusted to fit your Miniature American Shepherd.

11. **Broad Jump**. This obstacle will test your Miniature American Shepherd's ability to jump over several panels which have been laid out on the ground. While the panels are only inches above the ground, the width of the jump can vary according to your Miniature American Shepherd.

12. **Weave Poles**. All of us have seen videos of dogs snapping through Weave Poles at agility competitions. The poles are 2 feet apart, and depending on the competition, there will be between 6 and 12 poles. Weave Poles are the most challenging of obstacles. Your Miniature American Shepherd must begin its run through the poles on the right side and has to go around every one in sequence. Because of the strain Weave Poles can put upon a dog's body, take this obstacle slowly when training your

Miniature American Shepherd, and once again, make sure your Miniature American Shepherd's body is fully mature to help prevent fractures and other injuries.

Chapter Fourteen: Getting Your Miniature American Shepherd Started

Now that you understand what kinds of obstacles agility competitions will contain, and you have supplied yourself with the proper equipment, it's time to get started on training your Miniature American Shepherd (and yourself). Once again, if you haven't taught obedience to your Miniature American Shepherd yet, you absolutely must go back and train your Miniature American Shepherd adequately; a Miniature American Shepherd with no obedience training will simply be unable to master agility in a reasonable amount of time.

Your Miniature American Shepherd must also be able to respond positively to your commands when it is off leash – no leashes are allowed in agility, your Miniature American Shepherd will be reacting to your verbal and physical cues. If you have been teaching your Miniature American Shepherd tricks, you'll find that many of these will make teaching agility that much easier; if your Miniature American Shepherd already knows 'Jump', then transferring this to the different jumps required during an agility competition will be a snap.

As with puppies, Miniature American Shepherd adults will do better with the obstacles if they are introduced to them gradually. Get your Miniature American Shepherd used to walking on boards while they are still on the ground. If your Miniature American Shepherd slips off or jumps off, no harm will come to it at this point. Introduce your Miniature American Shepherd to one obstacle at a time, and only progress to the next once your Miniature American Shepherd is comfortable with the first.

When training for obstacles like your Dog Walk, raise the board incrementally off the ground until it is at the regulation height.

This will help your Miniature American Shepherd develop balance as the board gets higher and higher off the ground and help prevent acrophobia.

In addition to introducing your Miniature American Shepherd to the obstacles, it will also have to learn a new set of commands in order to successfully complete an agility course. It probably won't take as long for your Miniature American Shepherd to learn these as it was to learn commands initially since your Miniature American Shepherd is already used to responding to your directives.

1. Move. There is a time limitation to all competitive agility meets and regardless of how effectively your Miniature American Shepherd goes through the obstacles, they will either lose points or be disqualified if they are too slow. 'Move' is designed to give your Miniature American Shepherd a mental push to get it to run faster. Put your Miniature American Shepherd on leash and start out walking, speed up to a trot and say 'Move'. Progress to a run while giving the command.

2. Go. This cue will indicate to your Miniature American Shepherd which obstacle it must go to next. There is no set designation for obstacles at any agility competition; the obstacles can be arranged any way the organizers see fit. You can teach this either with a treat or a toy. Put your Miniature American Shepherd into a 'Stay', hold onto its collar, and then toss the treat or toy several feet away. Release your Miniature American Shepherd and say 'Go'. When you tell your Miniature American Shepherd 'Go' also point at the toy or treat, to accustom your Miniature American Shepherd to hand signals.

3. Up. You will need this cue for your Dog Walk and A-Frame. This cue will be especially easy to teach if you already allow your Miniature American Shepherd onto the furniture. Every time you see your Miniature American Shepherd heading

towards the couch or an armchair, as soon as it starts to jump, say 'Up'. You can also pat the furniture to draw your Miniature American Shepherd's interest. If your Miniature American Shepherd has been forbidden the furniture, you can substitute a box or a rock outside. Pat the box or rock and say 'Up'. If your Miniature American Shepherd doesn't jump up on its own, lift your Miniature American Shepherd onto the object, saying 'Up' as you do so.

4. Through. You will need to teach this command mostly for the tunnels, but it can also be useful for the jumping obstacles. (If your Miniature American Shepherd is already an ace at 'Jump' just stick to this command for the jumps.) You can make a short tunnel out of kitchen chairs and a sheet to get your Miniature American Shepherd used to the idea, or simply use an agility tunnel that has been compressed somewhat so that your Miniature American Shepherd can easily see the end. A helper can hold your Miniature American Shepherd at the opposite end while you wait with a treat at the other. Tell your Miniature American Shepherd 'Through' and wave the treat around so it can see it.

5. Tunnel. As your Miniature American Shepherd becomes familiar with the 'Through' command, it's time to help it identify the obstacle that it will be used for. Once your Miniature American Shepherd is reliably going through your tunnel on cue, start saying 'Tunnel' or 'Through Tunnel'. Linking the word 'tunnel' with the 'Through' command will make it easier for your Miniature American Shepherd to understand what you want.

6. Cross. Because you and your Miniature American Shepherd will be darting all over the obstacle course during a competition, there will be times when your Miniature American Shepherd will have to cross in front of you to reach the next challenge. This works best with a helper. Tell your Miniature American Shepherd 'Stay' and have your helper hold your Miniature American

Shepherd to your left. Throw a treat or toy to your right and have the helper let go of your Miniature American Shepherd as you say 'Cross'. Make sure you practice both right and left crosses.

7. Weave. Your 'Weave' command will let your Miniature American Shepherd know that it's time to go through the weave poles. The weave poles are probably the place where most dogs 'wash out' during a competition so make certain that your Miniature American Shepherd not only knows the 'Weave' command but will also respond to it quickly.

8. Plank. Your Miniature American Shepherd will have to navigate several obstacles that involve planks or boards, as we have detailed previously. Using one command for the A-Frame, Teeter-Totter, and Dog Walk can help simplify the process for your Miniature American Shepherd and make it more likely that it will act quickly on your command.

9. Slow. This command would prove to be useful if your Miniature American Shepherd may be taking some of the obstacles too enthusiastically, such as your Dog Walk. When the possibility of an injury exists because your Miniature American Shepherd is going too fast, teaching it the 'Slow' command is important. You can do this by trotting with your Miniature American Shepherd on leash, then slowing down to a walk and saying 'Slow'.

10. Jump. Since your Miniature American Shepherd probably already understands this command, it should be easy to transfer it from tricks to agility. Run your Miniature American Shepherd up to one of the jump obstacles, say 'Jump' and more than likely your Miniature American Shepherd will sail right over it. Don't make the jumps too high to begin with and always scale them to the height of your Miniature American Shepherd.

11. Chute. This command can be used when your Miniature American Shepherd will be going through the collapsed tunnel, or you can just use the 'Tunnel' command when approaching it.

If your Miniature American Shepherd is really quick to respond to learning new commands, then you can certainly add 'Chute', but if 'Tunnel' works just as well, stick with that.

12. Tire. One of the obstacles at an agility meet is a tire suspended within a framework. While the jump command could be used when running to the tire, giving the specific cue 'Tire' can help your Miniature American Shepherd focus on the target and could prevent confusion.

13. Table. Use 'Table' to get your Miniature American Shepherd onto the Pause Table, which will also involve sitting or lying down on it for approximately 5 seconds.

Once again, it cannot be stressed more that patience and positive reinforcement are the real keys to successful agility. Your Miniature American Shepherd is not trying to defy you when it doesn't comprehend what you want it to do, it just needs more time to learn. Any time you feel yourself becoming frustrated and angry is the time to stop the agility lessons. A dog that fears punishment, even if it's just a tongue lashing, will learn at a much slower rate just because its mind is on avoiding punishment, rather than the task at hand.

Take the lessons as slowly as your Miniature American Shepherd needs. Some Miniature American Shepherds will catch on almost immediately. However, nearly every Miniature American Shepherd that is physically able can become a star in its own way in agility. You may not have a Miniature American Shepherd that will be a competitor in agility trials, but you will have a Miniature American Shepherd that is having fun doing something with the person it loves most – you – and that is every bit as important as having a Miniature American Shepherd that wins blue ribbons.

If you have been using a clicker for training tricks and games, then continue to use it for agility. Also keep plenty of treats on hand; there are delicious, low calorie treats such as freeze-dried liver chunks that dogs love, and they won't add to your Miniature American Shepherd's waistline. Breaking up the training sessions with a bit of play also helps your Miniature American Shepherd learn agility more quickly and makes it more pleasant for both of you.

Another thing that can make a world of difference in agility trials is where you will be during the run. It's a good idea to decide now where you will be holding yourself in relation to your Miniature American Shepherd – will you have your Miniature American Shepherd on your left or on your right side? Choosing a side that is comfortable for you and sticking with it right from the start will help both of you navigate the obstacle course much more easily. The decision can be made simply on the basis of whether you are right- or left-handed.

Although you will not be able to use them in competitions, there are a few more items that can help to make agility training easier:

1. Targeting sticks are simply lightweight sticks about 3 feet long that you use to point out where you want your Miniature American Shepherd to go and say 'Table' for instance. Dogs tend to follow the direction in which you point naturally, so this can help your Miniature American Shepherd understand your directions more easily.

2. Targeting discs can also help your Miniature American Shepherd find its way through an agility course. Use a premade disc or simply use an old lid from a food container. Toss the disc where you want your Miniature American Shepherd to go, at the same time naming the obstacle.

3. Many people find that using a leash to help their dog through the obstacle course can make the learning process go faster initially. A leash will also keep your Miniature American Shepherd from taking off on its own once it's tired of the lessons or when something has drawn its attention. Don't reprimand

your Miniature American Shepherd in this case, either. If your Miniature American Shepherd is getting bored, continuing will be counterproductive. If your Miniature American Shepherd wants to chase the neighbor's cat, simply hold it by your side until it calms down and try going through the lesson again.

4. Keep attuned to your Miniature American Shepherd's attitude. Not only should you be alert for signs of boredom, but also for signs of stress. If your Miniature American Shepherd is laying back its ears or starting to tuck its tail, it's time to stop. Nervous head gestures or moving indecisively are also indicators that lessons are over. Your Miniature American Shepherd will learn much more quickly when it's relaxed and comfortable.

Starting with Jumps

Jumps are a good place to start when you begin agility training, there are numerous jumps on every agility field. We already covered the different kinds of jumps your Miniature American Shepherd can expect to find during a meet, so it's a good idea to set up a variety of jumps when you begin to train your Miniature American Shepherd.

Start with the jump at the lowest level, regardless of your Miniature American Shepherd's ability, to accustom your Miniature American Shepherd to it before raising higher. Don't overdo jump practice as it can increase the possibility of your Miniature American Shepherd becoming injured. Keep the sessions short to begin with to give your Miniature American Shepherd's body time to adjust to jumping.

1. Walk your Miniature American Shepherd through a short course of single jumps, giving the command 'Jump' as you approach the obstacle. If you are using a leash, abandon it as soon as possible; you will not be allowed to use a leash at a trial.

2. Once your Miniature American Shepherd is familiar with this, start going through the course at a trot. At this point you should not be using a leash at all, if you still find it necessary, go back to walking your Miniature American Shepherd through your course.

3. Raise the height of the jumps gradually as your Miniature American Shepherd becomes used to them.

4. Add in the broad jump and plank jump as your Miniature American Shepherd progresses.

Getting Used to the Tire

Because the tire jump is just another jump, it's best to add this now to your Miniature American Shepherd's training. Let the base of the tire rest on the ground to start.

1. Lead your Miniature American Shepherd up to the tire and say either 'Jump' or 'Tire', whichever command you have decided to use. Don't interchange the terms, choose one and stick with it.

2. As with the other jumps, walk your Miniature American Shepherd through it to begin with.

3. When your Miniature American Shepherd is reliably going through the tire from a walk, advance to a trot and then a run. (Some enthusiastic Miniature American Shepherds will want to take the tire jump at a run right from the start.)

4. Gradually raise the tire until it's at the correct height for your Miniature American Shepherd in competition.

5. Use tape to wrap the tire so that your Miniature American Shepherd's feet don't get caught when it's going through.

Dog Walk

There will definitely be a Dog Walk at every agility trial, so getting your Miniature American Shepherd used to this is absolutely essential. Using the command 'Up' will help to keep the instruction clear in your Miniature American Shepherd's mind, and using only one word will allow it to focus better. The three boards should be hinged so that there is no chance of them sliding out of place. It would probably be a good idea to teach your Miniature American Shepherd to use both slatted and smooth boards as either may be offered.

1. Lay the boards that will be used in your Dog Walk on the ground. The middle board can simply be flat at this time.

2. Lead your Miniature American Shepherd to one end of your Dog Walk and say 'Up' as you lead your Miniature American Shepherd onto the board.

3. Some Miniature American Shepherds may be afraid to step onto the boards, but you can overcome this by placing a line of treats on the board, or placing your Miniature American Shepherd partway down one of the boards. Hold your Miniature American Shepherd's leash so that it can't just step off. If your Miniature American Shepherd starts to back up to get off the board, let it, this will help it accustom itself to the board, too.

4. Once your Miniature American Shepherd is comfortable walking over the boards when they are resting on the ground, you can start to raise the middle one. Do this incrementally, and make sure that your Dog Walk is absolutely stable.

5. Let your Miniature American Shepherd walk over your Dog Walk once it has been raised to the regulation height of 4 feet, then gradually increase the pace. Keep your Miniature American Shepherd on leash as you proceed to trot and run to help stabilize it.

6. As soon as your Miniature American Shepherd is able to navigate your Dog Walk at a run without problems while on leash, you can take the leash off. If your Miniature American

Shepherd slows down initially when off leash on your Dog Walk, just give it time to gain confidence.

7. Don't hesitate to retrace steps if your Miniature American Shepherd is having problems; it's better to handle any problems slowly than to push your Miniature American Shepherd.

A-Frame

Because the A-Frame is another elevated obstacle that could potentially cause harm were your Miniature American Shepherd to fall from it, you should also take this one slowly. This is one of the more difficult obstacles for your Miniature American Shepherd to master, but any agile Miniature American Shepherd should be able to learn how to do it successfully. You will be using the command 'Up' again. Remember that you will be doing more pointing than speaking during a trial, so always combine your verbal command with the physical indication.

The A-Frame is relatively steep, so once again, begin with the obstacle flat or nearly flat on the ground. This will also help your Miniature American Shepherd get used to the slats that it will use for traction once the A-Frame is elevated. Always remember to make sure that at whatever the elevation of the A-Frame that it has been completely stabilized.

1. If your Miniature American Shepherd has already been working on your Dog Walk, it will probably not balk at walking over the A-Frame. You can even begin with the obstacle raised a few inches in the middle off the ground.

2. As your Miniature American Shepherd becomes more familiar with the A-Frame, gradually raise the center until it has reached the maximum height of 5' 6".

3. Train your Miniature American Shepherd to keep to the center of the A-Frame as much as possible to prevent it falling off while on the obstacle.

4. By starting the A-Frame at a very low level, you will help build up your Miniature American Shepherd's muscles to deal with what is actually climbing, as well as learning how to navigate the down side of the obstacle without losing its balance.

Tunnel

Teaching your Miniature American Shepherd to navigate the tunnel is not as difficult as you may think, especially if you have the assistance of a helper. Tunnels can vary between 10 and 20 feet.

1. Reduce the length of the tunnel as much as possible so that your Miniature American Shepherd can easily see the far end.

2. Have your helper hold your Miniature American Shepherd at one end of the tunnel while you squat near the other end.

3. Call your Miniature American Shepherd and hold out a treat, while giving the command 'Tunnel'. Your Miniature American Shepherd will most likely come right through the tunnel to you. If your Miniature American Shepherd hesitates, throw the treat about halfway down the tunnel to encourage your Miniature American Shepherd.

4. Once your Miniature American Shepherd is comfortable negotiating the short tunnel, lengthen it out, and when it will go through the longer tunnel confidently you can start adding curves.

5. Secure the tunnel in some way to make sure it doesn't roll while your Miniature American Shepherd is in it. This is ordinarily done with sandbags, but braces are also available that will hold the tunnel still.

Chute

Whether you use the cue 'Chute' or 'Tunnel' for this obstacle is up to you, just make certain that you choose one and stick with it.

1. If your Miniature American Shepherd is already familiar with the tunnel, it will probably be easier for it to learn how to go through the chute.

2. Use a helper to hold your Miniature American Shepherd at the open end while you station yourself at the collapsed fabric.

3. Because your Miniature American Shepherd will not realize that it can go through the fabric, in most cases, hold the cloth so that the end of the chute is only partially covered. Make sure that your Miniature American Shepherd can see you.

4. Call your Miniature American Shepherd with a 'Come' and as soon as it's released and making its way towards you, say 'Tunnel' (or 'Chute').

5. Lower the level of the fabric as the lesson is repeated, and finally leave the tunnel totally collapsed on the fabric end.

6. Lead your Miniature American Shepherd up to the open end at a run, give the command signal and your Miniature American Shepherd will probably run right through without problem.

Pause Table

Because they are so enthused about going through the course, many dogs get caught up on the Pause Table. After running fully out, your Miniature American Shepherd will be expected to jump onto the Pause Table, sit or lie down, and wait until given the cue to continue. This, of course, will really test a dog's training and self-control, but with practice, your Miniature American Shepherd will master the Pause Table, too.

1. Pat the table, say 'Table' to encourage your Miniature American Shepherd to get onto it. If your Miniature American Shepherd doesn't seem to understand, place a treat on the table and repeat until your Miniature American Shepherd will jump onto the table without problem.

2. When your Miniature American Shepherd is on the table say either 'Down' or 'Sit'. Your Miniature American Shepherd should comply with your command. Decide on one term to use and stay with it, going back and forth can confuse your Miniature American Shepherd and make it more likely that it will fail this part of the trial. In general, your Miniature American Shepherd will have to remain on the Pause Table from 5 to 10 seconds.

3. As your Miniature American Shepherd begins to respond better to its instructions and will reliably jump onto the table then become stationary, you will have to get it moving again. Use the 'Go' command to get your Miniature American Shepherd going and run along with it to give it the right idea.

Teeter-Totter

This can be one of the more difficult of the obstacles for your Miniature American Shepherd to get used to. The abrupt slamming motion when your pooch crosses the midpoint of the Teeter-Totter is off-putting to a lot of dogs. Because this obstacle can startle your Miniature American Shepherd, you may have to take this one very slowly and use plenty of treats. As there is always the danger of your Miniature American Shepherd falling off the Teeter-Totter, especially when moving at speed, it's vital that you help your Miniature American Shepherd develop the balance and confidence when dealing with this obstacle. To begin with, use a leash with your Miniature American Shepherd. You will be using the 'Go' command with this obstacle while pointing at it.

1. As you did with your Dog Walk and A-Frame, start off with your 'Teeter-Totter' nearly flat on the floor. Place a dowel under a board to serve as the fulcrum. Position the dowel so that the side your Miniature American Shepherd will be walking up on will already be on the floor or ground. Point to the board and say 'Go'.

2. Lead your Miniature American Shepherd on leash towards the fulcrum and let it step so that the board lowers in the direction your Miniature American Shepherd is facing.

3. Don't be surprised if your Miniature American Shepherd is startled to begin with, even with a relatively small drop, but the leash should prevent your Miniature American Shepherd leaving the board.

4. When your Miniature American Shepherd seems comfortable navigating the entire length of the Teeter-Totter, use a larger fulcrum. You can keep increasing the size, but always keep in mind that the Teeter-Totter must be absolutely stable to prevent accidents. If you make your own obstacle, make sure that it won't tip your Miniature American Shepherd off or collapse when your Miniature American Shepherd uses it. At this point, keep your Miniature American Shepherd on leash – this will not only serve to control your Miniature American Shepherd, but to make it feel more confident.

5. As you raise the height of the Teeter-Totter, watch to see whether your Miniature American Shepherd becomes startled at the sound when the board smacks down onto the floor. Keep an eye on your Miniature American Shepherd when this happens at first to make sure it doesn't try to bolt off the board to the side.

6. Once your Miniature American Shepherd can go from one side of the Teeter-Totter without problem on the leash, it's time to remove the leash. Point to the obstacle and say 'Go'.

7. To get your Miniature American Shepherd to speed things up on the Teeter-Totter, add the 'Move' command.

8. Some Miniature American Shepherds will be afraid of the Teeter-Totter regardless of how you have tried to train them. The problem here is usually that your Miniature American Shepherd is fearful of being on what seems to be an unsteady surface. The answer to this is a wobble board. Use a small object under a piece

of plywood that is large enough to accommodate your Miniature American Shepherd comfortably. A small object to start will allow the wobble board to move around, but not enough to alarm your Miniature American Shepherd. Increasing the size of the object as your Miniature American Shepherd develops its balance will help prepare it for the challenge of the Teeter-Totter.

Weave Poles

Weave Poles are probably the most difficult of the agility obstacles to teach to your Miniature American Shepherd. Remember, however, that thousands and thousands of dogs have been able to master this obstacle successfully, thanks to patience, positive reinforcement, and dedication on the part of their owners. You will achieve success more quickly when teaching the Weave Poles to your Miniature American Shepherd if you use a helper to begin with. It's probably best to use 'Weave' to get your Miniature American Shepherd going on this obstacle; this will help to distinguish it from the other obstacles and help your Miniature American Shepherd to focus on the poles. The point is to make it as simple as possible for your Miniature American Shepherd to navigate the obstacle course.

Remember, the Weave Poles should not be a part of your Miniature American Shepherd's repertoire until it is fully adult and the growth plates in the bones have fused. Permanent damage can be done to your Miniature American Shepherd's legs if you try to start teaching this obstacle while your Miniature American Shepherd is still a puppy. Keep in mind that limping dogs are not allowed to enter any agility competition.

1. Begin to teach the Weave Poles by spreading the poles apart to the sides so that your Miniature American Shepherd can simply walk through them as if it was walking between two walls. This will allow your Miniature American Shepherd to become familiar with the poles without actually having to twist and turn.

2. Your helper should hold onto your Miniature American Shepherd at one end of the Weave Poles while you walk through them.

3. Once you reach the far end of the Weave Poles, call your Miniature American Shepherd as your helper releases it.

4. As soon as your Miniature American Shepherd will come to you without hesitation, you can dispense with your human helper.

5. Place your Miniature American Shepherd in a 'Sit' and 'Stay' at one end of the spread poles. Go to the opposite end and pat your legs and use your chosen command word now. There should be no problem with your Miniature American Shepherd coming right to you.

6. As soon as your Miniature American Shepherd does this without problem, it's time to change the game a bit: after putting your Miniature American Shepherd in a 'Stay', walk on the outside of the spread poles and then call your Miniature American Shepherd. If your Miniature American Shepherd strays outside the poles, perhaps trying to follow in your footsteps, use a leash to lead it through the poles while you continue to walk on the outside.

7. Now it's time to start moving the poles closer together. Do this in small increments to make it easier for your Miniature American Shepherd. Make sure that you have set up the poles so that your Miniature American Shepherd enters them on the right side – conditioning your Miniature American Shepherd to feel the touch of the pole on its left shoulder will help teach your Miniature American Shepherd the right way to begin the Weave Poles.

8. You may have to use a leash once the poles begin to tighten up, and don't hesitate to use treats as well to help your Miniature American Shepherd understand what is required. Once again,

yelling or other signs of impatience are not only unnecessary, but counterproductive.

9. Don't wait until the weave poles have been placed in their correct position before you and your Miniature American Shepherd begin to take them at a run. Getting your Miniature American Shepherd to run through the poles while they are still some distance apart will make it easier and help to develop your Miniature American Shepherd's balance further.

10. Remember to begin every run with your target command word, 'Weave', and by pointing. Always make certain that your Miniature American Shepherd is beginning on the right side of the poles.

11. Should your Miniature American Shepherd be having difficulty in keeping on course after the poles have been put into a straight line, you can use guides to help keep your Miniature American Shepherd on course. These are flexible attachments for the poles that not only prevent your Miniature American Shepherd from leaving the obstacle, but that also keep your Miniature American Shepherd close to the poles.

12. If your Miniature American Shepherd is having trouble getting through 12 or 18 poles, why not start with a fewer number? Getting your Miniature American Shepherd to go through 4 or 6 poles successfully, then gradually working up the number can make it a lot easier for a dog that may be having difficulty. Don't hesitate to use the leash to guide your Miniature American Shepherd if it's having trouble.

Putting It All Together

Once your Miniature American Shepherd has learned each obstacle and will perform as required with only the command word and your hand signal, it's time to begin putting together an obstacle course to provide practice runs for you and your

Miniature American Shepherd. Always keep in mind that there is no 'set in stone' way that agility courses will be set up at trials, it is always at the discretion of the trial organizers. For this reason, it's a good idea to vary your course to accustom your Miniature American Shepherd to the vagaries of any particular meet.

If you haven't spent as much time as you should have in using hand signals, now is the time to conduct a crash course. You will need to rely on signaling your Miniature American Shepherd this way during a trial because in most cases, your Miniature American Shepherd will be outrunning you. To do this successfully, set up only a few obstacles at your home course and use only your hand and body language to get your Miniature American Shepherd to move.

Be patient if this is fairly new to your Miniature American Shepherd, but if you run along with your Miniature American Shepherd and use only hand signals to direct your Miniature American Shepherd, it should catch on quickly. Change the course around as you work on this and add more obstacles to familiarize your Miniature American Shepherd more thoroughly. And when you do use verbal commands, make sure that you 'bark' them out loudly and enthusiastically.

Call-Offs

It's probably inevitable that at some time during either training, or during a trial, that your Miniature American Shepherd will start to go to the wrong obstacle. As this can be an instant elimination in a trial, it's important that you teach your Miniature American Shepherd a command or two to direct it. You can simply use 'Here' and point to show your Miniature American Shepherd the correct route. You can teach this command by using the word and pointing where you want your Miniature American Shepherd to go. By this time, your Miniature American Shepherd has already learned so many commands that it should be easier for it to learn another one.

To further refine the call-off you can use the commands 'Go Right' and 'Go Left'. Teaching these commands will be especially important not only in reference to the Weave Poles, but also when your Miniature American Shepherd is at risk of taking the wrong direction after completing an obstacle. Most dogs will simply want to continue in a straight line towards the next obstacle, but if the next one in the course is to one side, or even out of your Miniature American Shepherd's line of sight, these directional commands can get your Miniature American Shepherd moving the right way.

There can be as many as 20 obstacles at an agility trial, so it's important for you to be in good physical condition, too, as you will have to run along with your Miniature American Shepherd. If you're a bit out of shape, this is the perfect time to condition yourself as well as help your Miniature American Shepherd prepare for an agility trial. Make sure that the clothes you choose are comfortable and will allow you freedom of movement. Your shoes should be lightweight, but provide good traction. If you have long hair, you may want to tie it back while running a course.

1. Begin by putting 2 or 3 of the obstacles in a line. A jump on either side of your Dog Walk is a good way to start.

2. Start to run with your Miniature American Shepherd, point at the first jump, and say 'Jump'.

3. As you approach your Dog Walk, give the 'Up' command and point as you run alongside.

4. Finish up with a 'Jump' at the last jump and then treat and praise your Miniature American Shepherd.

5. You can keep adding obstacles, but it's also a good idea to research online (and offline) for places that provide maps of 'official' obstacle courses at agility trials.

6. In order to help prepare your Miniature American Shepherd for a successful trial, change the order of the obstacles around – there is no 'set' pattern for agility trials.

Hopefully, everything has gone well for you and no insurmountable problems have arisen. However, it would be naïve to assume that every Miniature American Shepherd takes to agility smoothly; in fact the opposite is probably true in more cases than not. Should you find yourself having problems with agility training, don't hesitate to seek out the services of a professional trainer. Don't just drop your Miniature American Shepherd off, either, stay with it so that you can learn how to train and support it. Obviously, it's perfectly possible to teach your Miniature American Shepherd agility on your own, and many people consider this to be the best way to do so, but if you are having some problems or simply don't have enough time, don't hesitate to enroll your Miniature American Shepherd with a trainer.

Although there are a few organizations that offer cash prizes for success in agility trials, most do not, but few people participate in agility with their dogs for financial gain, they are simply competing for fun. Accumulating ribbons, medals, and trophies, however, shows how well you and your Miniature American Shepherd are doing in this sport.

Chapter Fifteen: Getting Involved in Agility

Once you have done all you can to train your Miniature American Shepherd in agility (or participated in trainer-run agility classes), you might feel that it's time to get actively involved. There are actually two ways to start agility competitions: matches and trials. Regardless of how well you and your Miniature American Shepherd have performed to date, it's probably a good idea to start with matches.

Agility Matches

If you have not yet joined a local agility club, this is probably an excellent time to do so. Local agility clubs will generally allow puppies as young as 4 months old (just when you would be starting training) to participate in matches. If you do start with a local club when your Miniature American Shepherd is a puppy, it will not only learn agility safely, but will also have a great chance to become socialized with the other pets there. The puppy will also become accustomed to being around larger numbers of people, reducing the chance of nervousness during a trial.

Another plus to matches is that they are open not only to pure-breed dogs, but also to mixed-breeds, which are denied participation in many competitive trials. Mixed breed dogs can be every bit as good at agility as pure-breed dogs, so this will give your favorite 'mutt' a chance to shine too.

Keep in mind, however, that your work in matches will not be used as any kind of official recognition with regards to competitive trials. There are no certificates or ribbons given at matches that will increase your standing at any trial, but matches are still an excellent way to practice, help your Miniature American Shepherd adult or puppy become socialized, and meet new people. There is much less pressure at matches, with the emphasis being on having fun. Many people never go any further than matches.

Competitive Trials

If you have joined a local agility club and you and your Miniature American Shepherd have done well at matches, you may well consider moving on to competitive trials. Trials have a much more structured format than do matches. Dogs younger than 12 months, or in some cases 18 months, will not be allowed in them as they are much more rigorous than matches.

Also unlike matches, if you want to participate in a trial you will have to register well in advance. You will then receive a list of trials that will be available, and depending on your financial situation (there are fees associated with Competitive Trials as well as any possible travel costs) and available time, you will be able to arrange a trial schedule for you and your Miniature American Shepherd. In order for your Miniature American Shepherd's agility trials to 'count' as far as progression in the sport goes, you will need to enroll in trials that are run by certain agility clubs. For those in the United States, the American Kennel Club (AKC) is a good place to start for trial information. If you live in the United Kingdom, the United Kennel Club (UKC) sponsors trials.

Junior Class Agility

Kids and dogs are naturals together, and one of the best ways to learn agility with your Miniature American Shepherd is to start out young. The AKC sponsors classes and events for children and their dogs not only to keep interest alive in agility, but also to help children learn the proper way to train their dogs. These classes are also a great way for kids to learn the principles of sportsmanship. The classes offered are called AKC Junior Showmanship Classes and they are divided into 3 categories:

1. The Junior Class is for children who are no younger than 9 years old, but not yet 12.

2. The Intermediate Class is designed for kids between the ages of 12 and 14.

3. The Senior Class is for youths who are 15 years old, but have not yet turned 18.

The division of classes by age group will help less experienced children gain confidence in handling their Miniature American Shepherd during an agility trial. There are some regulations that must be met: your Miniature American Shepherd being presented by the child must either be the child's dog or the family dog; your Miniature American Shepherd has to meet the age requirements; children and their dogs must dress and behave appropriately. Most local dog clubs will offer junior memberships. It's often a good idea for youngsters interested in dog agility to attend some Junior Class Agility shows; this will give them a chance to see firsthand how a trial is conducted and also get acquainted with children who are already active in agility.

Other agility clubs for children and teens will have different requirements, with some children as young as 5 being permitted to join. Most agility clubs will provide training classes.

Chapter Sixteen: The Agility Trial

The Rules

Perhaps before you begin actively training your Miniature American Shepherd in agility, you should familiarize yourself with exactly what is required at an agility meet. This can help to avoid disappointment and frustration. As stated before, the obstacle course arrangement will vary from trial to trial, although all of the obstacles will be used. There are a few general rules that will apply at every agility trial:

1. No food or treats are allowed during the trial

2. Not only is a leash not allowed, but your Miniature American Shepherd will not be allowed to wear a collar.

3. The handler is not allowed to touch your Miniature American Shepherd at any time during its run on the course.

4. You will be allowed to walk through the course before the competition starts. You will have to do your best to memorize the correct way to navigate the course, and will be given about 10 minutes to do so.

Keep in mind that there are always entry fees with agility trials and these are not generally refundable. The costs of competing can run up considerably if you have to travel long distances to get to the show: you will have lodging fees to contend with, as well as the normal costs associated with travel such as fuel costs. Keep in mind that if you have to rent a vehicle to attend a trial, that will also add to your total expenditure. Should you be traveling away from your home base, ask your veterinarian for a recommendation on a vet near where the trial will be taking place; it's better to know where to take your Miniature American Shepherd ahead of time should illness or injury occur.

There are certain basic things that you should bring with you to any agility trial: a crate for your Miniature American Shepherd with a pad or blanket for the bottom; a blanket to cover the crate to help keep it cooler; your Miniature American Shepherd's water dish, paper cups, and a supply of clean water; a chair for you to sit on; a hat; collar and leash. These should help to keep you and your Miniature American Shepherd comfortable during the competition. Do not neglect to bring along the means to clean up after your Miniature American Shepherd: a pooper scooper or appropriate bags.

You may also have to present your Miniature American Shepherd's vaccination record at the show, so be sure that you have a copy with you, your veterinarian should be happy to provide you with one. Even if a particular event does not require that you show proof of your Miniature American Shepherd's vaccinations, you should make certain that your Miniature American Shepherd is up to date on all of them – your Miniature American Shepherd will be around a lot of other dogs, so it's up to you to make sure that it has adequate protection. Because Kennel Cough spreads so easily, make sure that your Miniature American Shepherd has received this vaccination as well (this is an easy one, drops are simply put into your Miniature American Shepherd's nose).

Always remember that old maxim for travelers, "Take half the clothing you think you will need and twice the money." I have found myself that these are wise words and have served me very well when traveling, especially to a foreign country.

Speed Counts

Dogs are judged at an agility trial not only for their ability to navigate all the obstacles correctly, but also for the speed at which they do so. Adjustment is made with regards to the size of your Miniature American Shepherd, but regardless of the class, the fastest dog that completes the obstacle course correctly will be the winner. This is why it is important that you encourage your Miniature American Shepherd to take the obstacles as quickly as is safely possible.

Your Miniature American Shepherd will probably slow up a bit on your Dog Walk and Teeter-Totter, which is why it's a good idea to get your Miniature American Shepherd to move as quickly as they can on jumps, tunnel, and chute. During a trial you will understand the value of having taught your Miniature American Shepherd to go where you point and to listen to your commands – your Miniature American Shepherd will inevitably run faster than you, and by keeping it on course verbally and by pointing, you can really cut seconds off your run, especially if your Miniature American Shepherd is somewhat slow on your Dog Walk or Teeter-Totter. There is also a time limit on the run that your Miniature American Shepherd must keep within.

How Trials and Meets Are Conducted

When you begin to participate in agility with your Miniature American Shepherd, you will probably begin with meets. These are qualifying contests that will help you and your Miniature American Shepherd progress to the more challenging and prestigious trials. Dog clubs, such as the American Kennel Club (AKC), sponsor these trials. There are now literally thousands of meets and trials every year in countries around the world, and for those living in the United States or United Kingdom, it should not be difficult to find a meet appropriate for you.

To begin with, most agility organizations provide divisions to make the competition fairer in relation to breed and experience. These designations are meant to make the trials open to more people and their dogs and encourage participation. Keep in mind that no dog younger than 1 year of age will be allowed in an agility trial; some trials bar dogs younger than 18 months.

1. Novice class is for beginners in agility and offers a shorter course. This trial must be completed successfully, and your Miniature American Shepherd must have received a Novice title in order to go on to the next category. The pace of the course will be more at a trot rather than at a run.

2. Intermediate (Open) agility is for dogs that have been certified for the Novice class. The course is longer and more challenging than it is for the novices. At this level, your Miniature American Shepherd and its handler are expected to run through the course. This course is also longer than that for novices.

3. Advanced (Master or Elite) agility class is open for dogs that have received their Intermediate title. Not only will there be a stricter time limit, but the handler must stay farther away from their dog and communicate with it mostly by using hand signals.

4. Veterans class is open to older dogs, and gives these dogs a chance to show just how well an older dog can function. Jumps or hurdles will probably be set at a lower height, and the time limitations will not be as strict. A shorter obstacle course can also be offered.

In order to put your Miniature American Shepherd into the proper classification, measurements are taken for height at their shoulders (the withers). This will not only have bearing on how high the jumps will be set, but also for the timing of the course. Some trials will disqualify dogs if they fail to complete the course within a certain period of time while others will simply grade your Miniature American Shepherd, and award a fault, if it is too slow.

Faults

Faults are, in effect, black marks against your Miniature American Shepherd during the trial. Different organizations can have different designation of faults, and while some trials will simply keep track of the faults, others will immediately disqualify your Miniature American Shepherd if it commits one. A trial where the faults are simply noted and go towards lowering your Miniature American Shepherd's overall performance score is called a 'qualifying run'. These can be helpful in letting you know where your Miniature American Shepherd's weaknesses may lie, rather than being kicked off the field immediately. If your Miniature American Shepherd completes the course without being faulted, it will be said to have had a 'clean run'. Disqualification is why it's so important to make sure that your Miniature American Shepherd has been well trained in every aspect of agility, because the rules are strict.

Although each agility club will have specific errors that will be considered faults, you can expect your Miniature American Shepherd to be faulted on any combination of the following:

1. A Missed Contact can mean that your Miniature American Shepherd has not done an obstacle at all, or it can mean that it has not completed the obstacle. For instance, if your Miniature American Shepherd refuses to complete the Teeter-Totter or runs through the Pause Table, these are considered to be Missed Contacts.

2. A Knocked Bar will also constitute a fault. This can occur when your Miniature American Shepherd doesn't jump high enough and knocks the bar or plank on any of the jumps off its support.

3. A Refusal comes about when your Miniature American Shepherd simply refuses to tackle the obstacle in any way; dogs that will not enter the Tunnel or back away from a Jump will be faulted, and often will be disqualified immediately.

4. A Time Fault occurs when your Miniature American Shepherd has taken longer than is allowed for the completion of the obstacle course.

5. If your Miniature American Shepherd goes Off Course, by either one of your errors, it will be faulted.

6. A Weave Pole Fault occurs when your Miniature American Shepherd enters the Weave Poles on the left side, misses poles, or back-weaves to try to correct its error.

7. A Flyoff fault means that your Miniature American Shepherd has sailed off your Dog Walk or other elevated obstacle.

8. A Handling fault occurs if you touch your Miniature American Shepherd during the trial. Whether this was deliberate or accidental makes no difference, it is still a fault.

9. Unsportsmanlike behavior on the part of your Miniature American Shepherd's owner is considered a fault. This can include not only arguing with the judges, but also yelling at or striking your Miniature American Shepherd if it doesn't perform as you would like. Arguments with other contestants will also be a fault.

10. Defecating or urinating on the course will usually get a dog disqualified.

11. A Run-Out fault means that your Miniature American Shepherd has run off the course entirely.

12. Training in the Ring encompasses exactly what it states – the owner is trying to instruct your Miniature American Shepherd during the trial, rather than simply accompanying your Miniature American Shepherd.

Depending on the rules in effect at any particular trial, all of the above faults can mean instant elimination from the trial, or simply a demarcation. Because defecating or urinating during the trial is almost always an elimination, make sure that your Miniature American Shepherd has had a chance to walk off its latest drink and meal, and it's also advisable not to feed your Miniature American Shepherd generously right before the trial begins; a full stomach and/or bladder, combined with excitement can lead to trouble and your Miniature American Shepherd's disqualification.

And you should never forget that the best-trained Miniature American Shepherd can sometimes just have a bad day. Dogs can become overexcited easily, especially around other dogs and when exposed to crowds, noise, and a multitude of people. If your Miniature American Shepherd does mess up an agility trial and is eliminated, just chalk it up to experience. There is absolutely no excuse for punishing a dog that has ruined up its run; in most cases your Miniature American Shepherd will be fine at the next trial. However, if your Miniature American Shepherd seems off in anyway, check it carefully for even small injuries – an infected toenail can cause a dog to refuse obstacles or run off course.

Being eliminated from an agility trial is not the end of the world, be sure you put this into perspective. In fact, over handling by the owner, providing a windmill of hand and arm signals and a chorus of verbal commands could well be at the bottom of the problem as your Miniature American Shepherd may well have simply become confused by what you were trying to tell it.

Chapter Seventeen: Progressing Beyond Standard Agility

It may be true that most people who enter their Miniature American Shepherds into competitive agility trials tend to stick with Standard Agility, but there are a number of different trials available that add some spice and variety to agility trials. These competitions are often considered to be games, and are generally conducted at a faster pace than ordinary.

1. Jumping Class is just that; most of the obstacles will consist of jumps, although sometimes Weave Poles, Tunnel, and Chute are included. During this trial, your Miniature American Shepherd will be encouraged to run and jump as quickly as possible over the course. There will be no Dog Walk, Teeter-Totter, or Pause Table – this class is all about speed. As always, there will be a time limit and your Miniature American Shepherd and its handler must follow the correct path through the course.

2. The Gambler's Class (Joker or Jackpot Class) presents your Miniature American Shepherd and its handler with a two part trial. During the first part of the trial, the handler is actually free to direct your Miniature American Shepherd onto whatever obstacles he or she chooses. Since all obstacles are awarded a certain number of points for a successful completion, it's possible for a dog to really rack up points on those obstacles on which it excels. A buzzer or whistle signals the finish of the first part of the trial and now your Miniature American Shepherd will have to follow a pre-determined course of obstacles. This part is called the gamble, and the owner must signal its Miniature American Shepherd from a distance. The gamble is a difficult trial and usually only your Miniature American Shepherds that are the most experienced in agility will take part in it.

3. The Snooker Class trials depend on colored tags being set up on the obstacles. Although blue and red tags are those most frequently used, there is no limit to the colors or color combinations that can be placed on the obstacles. Additionally, each obstacle will have a numerical designation on it. In order to complete a Snooker Class course successfully, you and your Miniature American Shepherd will have to begin with, say, a blue obstacle that has '1' on it. After completing that obstacle, your Miniature American Shepherd will have to go to another blue obstacle, but this time one that runs from '2' to '7'. Your Miniature American Shepherd racks up points according to the number on the obstacle. This is probably the most confusing of trials and only dogs and owners who can work together perfectly as an agility team will be able to complete it successfully. This is not a trial for the faint of heart.

4. Team or Relay Class involves several teams of dogs and their owners. When 2 teams run the course, it is referred to as Relay Pairs, when there are 3 teams, or more, then the Relay Class is called Relay Teams. Depending on the rules set up by the sponsoring organization, a team might run part of a course before switching to another team or one team can finish the entire course, then allow the next team to take over.

5. The Power and Speed Class involves 2 parts. The first part of the course will consist of the A-Frame, Pause Table, Dog Walk, Broad Jump, and Weave Poles (the contact obstacles). This part will not be subject to a time limitation, but your Miniature American Shepherd must run a perfect course without getting any faults. If you and your Miniature American Shepherd, have managed to get a clean run, it will be time for the Speed Class. The Speed Class only has jumps in it, and this course is timed. The object is for your Miniature American Shepherd to go over or through all of the jumps in the shortest possible amount of time.

The above challenging agility trials can make agility even more fun for you and your Miniature American Shepherd. When you first began standard agility, you probably took things slowly to allow your Miniature American Shepherd to become accustomed to them; the same thing applies here. Go at a pace that your Miniature American Shepherd finds comfortable to start with, then 'up the ante' as confidence and skill builds. If you are not using a trainer, put together the appropriate course in your backyard and practice with your Miniature American Shepherd. For those of you who want to try Team or Relay Class trials, your local agility club will be able to match you up with like-minded people. Always make certain that your Miniature American Shepherd is in top physical condition before advancing to these challenging objectives, and be vigilant for any sign of injury.

Chapter Eighteen: Agility Is Not Without Risk

Injuries

While we are all familiar with sports injuries that humans suffer, dogs are also subject to the same kind of injuries, and there can be no denying that agility contributes in no small measure to this. In the United States alone, approximately 1,000,000 dogs compete in agility trials each year, so it's not surprising that there will be injuries incurred by some of the participants. Some of the injuries are mild, of course, but some are serious and can cause permanent damage to your Miniature American Shepherd. There is no reason to forego agility because of a fear of injuring your Miniature American Shepherd, but anyone who is starting to participate in this sport should be aware of the potential for harm.

1. Sprains and muscle strains were the most frequently observed injuries, along with bruising. Yes, your Miniature American Shepherd can get bruised, its hair simply hides the injury.

2. Nearly 1/3 of dogs who are in agility become injured, and this is not only at trials, the rate of injury for home-based agility exercises is identical to the statistics for matches and trials.

3. Most of the injuries involved the feet, shoulders, spine, and neck.

4. Normal veterinary care after an injury can help prevent repeat injuries. Owners who relied on 'alternative' care such as massage and acupuncture were more likely to see their dogs injured again.

5. Approximately half of the injuries healed up within a month's time, while the other half required 2 months or more for the injury

to heal. A small percentage of injuries resulted in permanent disability.

6. Although they are the most popular breed for agility, Border Collies were also the most likely to get hurt.

7. Not surprisingly, inexperienced dogs trained by inexperienced owners had higher rates of injury than people and dogs with several years of agility experience.

8. Any dog at an agility trial is more likely to be hurt when navigating your Dog Walk, Teeter-Totter, A-Frame, and any of the jumps.

Because intensive agility is a relative newcomer in the dog world, research is still being done to determine how best to treat many of the injuries so that your Miniature American Shepherd can return to the field as quickly as possible, and also how to prevent injuries from occurring in the first place. It is now recommended that any dog taking part in agility trials undergo a complete veterinary examination every 6 months, regardless of age, and even if your Miniature American Shepherd appears to be in perfect health. Dogs that have recovered from an injury should not only be examined before their next trial, but also every 3 months since previous injuries make it more likely that another injury will occur. Being aware of some of the more common injuries and familiarity with their treatment can help your Miniature American Shepherd stay active in agility.

Warm-Up Exercises Before a Trial

In the same way that human athletes need to warm up before a competition, so do canine athletes. If you take the time to warm your Miniature American Shepherd up before it starts its trial, the chances are that not only will your Miniature American Shepherd be less likely to get injured, but it will also give you a much better performance. You should set aside about half an hour before your Miniature American Shepherd is scheduled to compete to giving it a warm-up. The first step in this will be a 15 minute walk. This will get your Miniature American Shepherd's blood moving and start supplying more oxygen to the muscles. As more blood (and oxygen) arrives into the muscles, they become warmer and better able to handle stress. The warmed muscle will be able to respond much more quickly and will have a higher level of elasticity.

Besides giving your Miniature American Shepherd a walk, you can also help it to warm up effectively by having it go through some of the basic obedience commands. Tell your Miniature American Shepherd to 'Sit' and then tell it 'Down'. Repeating this several times will help loosen up the joints. As with walking your Miniature American Shepherd, this helps to get the joints and muscles warmed up nicely.

Stretching is particularly important as regards the shoulders, neck, and back; many of the agility injuries happen in these places. No, you will not be able to tell your Miniature American Shepherd to stretch while it starts doing so - you will have to help your Miniature American Shepherd stretch. Take your Miniature American Shepherd's right front leg and gently stretch it out; hold it in that position for several seconds and then return it to normal. You should do this about 5 times on each side. The same can be done for the hind legs. Just remember to use a smooth, gentle motion and avoid jerking your Miniature American Shepherd's legs.

You should also help your Miniature American Shepherd stretch its neck. You can do this by gently pushing your Miniature American Shepherd's head to the side until it touches the shoulders (don't force this, if you feel any real resistance, desist immediately), but a better way is to use a treat to tempt your Miniature American Shepherd to move its head in the desired direction itself. Do this 5 times on either side, and alternating sides will be especially beneficial.

Besides increasing circulation and warming the muscles and joints, warm-up exercises also help both you and your Miniature American Shepherd to relax. A relaxed dog will be less likely not only to make mistakes, but will also be less likely to be injured.

Common Agility Injuries

It will be almost inevitable that at some point, your Miniature American Shepherd will be injured while running the obstacle course. You will have to be diligent in watching for even the slightest of hurts, and treat them before they become more serious problems. While limping is probably the most obvious sign that something is wrong, other signs will include a hunched appearance, refusal of food and water, and even unexpected aggression from a good-natured dog.

1. Foot injuries are very common for dogs taking part in agility; your Miniature American Shepherd will be landing with some force every time it jumps over an obstacle, and even the rapid twisting going through the Weave Poles can result in injury. Damage to the footpad can be from lacerations or a puncture. Deep cuts to the footpad will require a visit to the vet. Your Miniature American Shepherd's nails can also get caught on obstacles (a good reason for keeping your Miniature American Shepherd's nails trimmed), or can be injured when your Miniature American Shepherd lands from a jump.

2. When your Miniature American Shepherd lands after completing an obstacle, not only will the footpads take some punishment, but also the front legs. Dogs can suffer damage to the carpal tendon, which could necessitate surgery. Other problems include damage to the knee and elbow, including causing a luxating patella and various other tendon injuries. Tendonitis, if

not severe, can be cured by rest and medication, but if the tendon is badly torn, surgery will be required.

3. Shoulder injuries can also occur during a trial. The first sign will be that your Miniature American Shepherd starts limping. The ball-and-socket joint of the shoulder can be injured, sprained, but the muscle extending from the elbow to the shoulder can also become strained. Using an ice pack (no more than 15 minutes at a time, with the pack wrapped in a towel) can help reduce inflammation and also lessen the chances that surgery will be required. Fortunately, it's been found that even if surgery is necessary, in the majority of cases your pooch should be able to return to agility after recuperation is complete.

4. Your Miniature American Shepherd's spine will also be taking some stress during an agility match or trial. The twists and turns of the Weave Poles and the convoluted path that must be followed through the obstacle course can cause spinal problems. Dogs can suffer from ruptured discs, just like people, and compression fractures can also occur. Compression fractures occur when the discs are jammed together suddenly; one of our Miniature American Shepherds has a compression fracture in his neck. It didn't affect him too much when he was younger, but now makes it difficult for him to jump onto furniture – he has to be lifted up.

5. Hip injuries are also possible from agility work. Twisting, landing hard after a jump, or scrunching down to get through the Tunnel or Chute can put strain on the hip joints. It should go without saying that any Miniature American Shepherd with hip dysplasia should not be in agility, but overuse of agility, especially when your Miniature American Shepherd has not had the chance to build up the proper muscles and accustom itself to the movements required, can also cause problems.

6. The same kind of tendon and muscle injuries that can occur on the front legs of your Miniature American Shepherd can

also occur on the back legs. The kneecap and elbow can become injured, as well as the paws and footpads. It's a good idea to check not only the toe - and footpads before and after a run, but between the toes as well to make certain that your Miniature American Shepherd has not picked up a small pebble, twig, or thorn.

Although there is a chance that your Miniature American Shepherd might become injured to one degree or another performing at agility, there is no reason to forego the sport either. Refraining from pushing your Miniature American Shepherd too hard, allowing a puppy to mature before diving into the more challenging obstacles, using warm-ups to prepare your Miniature American Shepherd for the trial, and watching carefully for even the slightest of injuries can all keep your Miniature American Shepherd active in agility.

Have Fun!

Agility should be all about having fun with your Miniature American Shepherd, and by conducting it in a relaxed manner will not only make it more enjoyable for both of you, but it will help prevent injuries from occurring in the first place. Competition is a big part of agility, but never lose sight of the other aspects of the sport: bonding more closely with your Miniature American Shepherd, meeting like-minded people, working towards a goal, and simply having fun.

While there will be some minor injuries that the owner will be able to address him - or herself, if the injury seems more serious, or you have any doubts, make sure to take your Miniature American Shepherd to the veterinarian as soon as possible. Keep in mind that even minor hurts can become serious if they are not treated in a timely manner.

Also remember that some injuries will take weeks or months to heal completely, and that some Miniature American Shepherds will never be able to compete again. The fact that your Miniature American Shepherd can be seriously hurt or will be unable to attend agility trials again are why it is so important to train it carefully and never push or force. Stay vigilant for any sign of injury, regardless of how slight it seems, and attend to it immediately. Never force a dog that is limping or seems to be in pain back onto the field.

Finally, remember to have fun, and continue to grow a loving bond with your Miniature American Shepherd.

www.ingramcontent.com/pod-product-compliance
Lightning Source LLC
Chambersburg PA
CBHW030441010526
44118CB00011B/736